'Wroughte in gold and silk'

PRESERVING THE ART OF
HISTORIC TAPESTRIES

*Anita Quye, Kathryn Hallett
and Concha Herrero Carretero*

In association with

National Museums Scotland

**Historic Royal
PALACES**

PATRIMONIO NACIONAL

First published in 2009 by
NMS Enterprises Limited – Publishing
a division of NMS Enterprises Limited
National Museums Scotland
Chambers Street
Edinburgh EH1 1JF
www.nms.ac.uk

Text: Anita Quye
© Trustees of National Museums Scotland 2009

Text: Kathryn Hallett
© Historic Royal Palaces 2009

Text: Concha Herrero Carretero
© Patrimonio Nacional 2009

Images © 2009, as credited;
and see Acknowledgements page below.

**British Library Cataloguing in
Publication Data**
A catalogue record for this book
is available from the British Library.

ISBN: 978 1 905267 15 6

Publication layout and design by
    NMS Enterprises Limited – Publishing.
Cover design by Mark Blackadder.
Cover image (front) of *Canillas seda y lana*
    (© Concha Herrero Carretero); (back) [PNM9]
    Wine Arbours Gallery (1660) [detail] by Jacob
    Wauters, Antwerp (active 1619-60)
    (© Patrimonio Nacional).
Printed in Great Britain by Butler Tanner & Dennis,
    Frome, Somerset.

Published by National Museums Scotland as one of
a series of titles based on museum scholarship and
partnership.

NOTE: *Colour variation between tapestry images reproduced in this book is due to photography having taken
place at different times and in various locations. The
colours are therefore not necessarily accurate for each
tapestry or its details.*

For a full listing of NMS Enterprises Limited –
Publishing titles and related merchandise:

shop.nms.ac.uk

Contents

Acknowledgements and Biographical Information

PROJECT ACKNOWLEDGEMENTS

The research project 'Monitoring of Damage in Historic Tapestries' was supported by the European Community under the Fifth Framework Programme and contributed to the implementation of the Key Action 'The City of Tomorrow and Cultural Heritage' through the subsection 'Improved Damage Assessment of Cultural Heritage' within the Energy, Environment and Sustainable Development Programme, contract number EVK4-CT-2001-00048. The authors are solely responsible for the content of this publication, which does not represent the opinion of the European Commission. The Commission is not responsible for any use that might be made of data appearing within this publication.

Support for Patrimonio Nacional's involvement in the project is gratefully acknowledged from Yago Pico de Coaña y Valicourt (Presidente de Patrimonio), José Antonio Bordallo Huidobro (Gerente de Patrimonio Nacional), and Juan Carlos de la Mata González (Director de Actuaciones Histórico-Artísticas).

IMAGE CREDITS

Listed below are the sources of illustrative material and images within this publication. No reproduction of material in copyright is permitted without prior contact with the publisher or owner of copyright.

BIRBECK COLLEGE, UNIVERSITY OF LONDON
Image copyright: © Birbeck College – for Appendix A.6

BRUGES MUSÉES COMMUNAUX /
BRUGES MUSÉE NOTRE-DAME DE LA POTERIE
Image copyright: © 2009 Museum Bruges – images courtesy of Reproductiefonds, for pp. 29-31

© CONCHA HERRERO CARRETERO – for the image on the front cover

HISTORIC ROYAL PALACES
Image copyright: © Historic Royal Palaces
for figures 2.3, 2.4, 2.5, 2.6, 2.13, 3.2, 3.3, 3.4, 3.5, 3.6, 3.7, 4.1, 4.4, 4.5, 4.6, 4.7, 5.1, 5.2, 5.3, 5.5, 5.6, 5.8, Appendix A.3 and A.4

© INGRID DE MEÛTER – for images on p. 28

© KATHRYN HALLETT
for pages 1 and 2 (see figure 2.7)

Monitoring of Damage in Historic Tapestries (MODHT Project)
Image copyright: © MODHT for figures 1.1, 1.2, 4.2 and 4.3

BIOGRAPHICAL INFORMATION

INES CASTELLANO-COLMENERO

Assistant Librarian at National Museums Scotland,
Edinburgh, Scotland.

DR MAREI HACKE

A scientist specialising in polymeric materials in the
Department of Conservation and Scientific Research,
British Museum, London.

KATHRYN HALLETT

Preventative Conservation and Science Manager,
Historic Royal Palaces, Hampton Court, England.

DR CONCHA HERRERO CARRETERO

Co-ordinator of the Conservation Department,
Patrimonio Nacional, Madrid, Spain.

DR DAVID HOWELL

Head of Conservation and Collection Care Service,
Bodleian Library, Oxford; and formerly a conservation scientist specialising in fibre analysis and
environmental monitoring in the Textile Conservation
Studios, Historic Royal Places, London.

DR MARIANNE ODLYHA

Director of Physical Sciences Programme and
Thermal Analysis Laboratory Manager, Birkbeck
College, University of London.

DR DAVID PEGGIE

Assistant Organic Analyst in the Scientific Department of the National Gallery, London.

DR ANITA QUYE

Principal Scientist at National Museums Scotland,
Edinburgh, Scotland.

INA VANDEN BERGHE

A scientist specialising in paper, leather and parchment in the Laboratories Department, Royal Institute
for Cultural Heritage (IRPA/KIK), Brussels.

Foreword

Jane Carmichael
NATIONAL MUSEUMS SCOTLAND

FOR most people tapestries offer an insight into the past, often combining imagery, beauty and practicality; for conservators they offer a complex challenge requiring understanding and patience. National Museums Scotland was pleased to be one of the partners in the European-Union funded project, 'Monitoring of Damage in Historic Tapestries' (MODHT), and we are delighted to support this publication. The project team learned a great deal through their collaborative working which has already been shared with the profession and benefited their respective collections. This publication brings together their research and marks their very tangible legacy. If it encourages professional confidence in caring for and exhibiting what can be regarded as 'difficult' museum objects, it will have achieved its aim.

Director of Collections
NATIONAL MUSEUMS SCOTLAND
April 2009

Foreword

Sir Hugh Roberts
THE ROYAL COLLECTION

THIS publication marks the conclusion of the highly significant MODHT project which has involved seven partners across Europe in the most intensive study yet undertaken to evaluate scientifically the cumulative damage to historic tapestries on permanent display.

The team of conservators and conservation scientists at Historic Royal Palaces, with whom the project originated, has been at the forefront of tapestry conservation in the United Kingdom for many years, and has the specific responsibility of caring for the most significant group of early tapestries in an historically associated setting anywhere in the United Kingdom.

As a result of the work carried out for this project, curators and conservators can now be guided in their decision-making in a way that would not have been possible in the past. While we no longer need to re-issue Henry VIII's Household Regulation that 'no man wipe their hands upon none arras of the kinges whereby they might be hurted', this significant publication gives us hope that the pace of scientific advance can match the natural and inevitable decay of all organic matter, and that judiciously planned and executed preventive conservation should be able – as least as far as tapestries are concerned – to slow this process down to a remarkable degree.

Director
THE ROYAL COLLECTION
April 2009

Foreword

Yago Pico de Coaña y Valicourt
PATRIMONIO NACIONAL

THE participation of Patrimonio Nacional (Crown Heritage) in the project 'Monitoring of Damage in Historic Tapestries' (MODHT) has meant the addition to it of one of the most valuable and substantial historic European collections – that assembled during the sixteenth and seventeenth centuries by the monarchs of the House of Habsburg or House of Austria in Spain, and now preserved in the Palacio Real, Madrid.

The selection of tapestries from this collection – illustrative of the art of tapestry and of the production from the most excellent workshops of Brussels, Bruges and Antwerp – was the objective of MODHT's first meeting on 7 October 2002 at the Palacio Real. The sampling that followed was essential to carry out physicochemical tests, and to assess the composition and characterisation of the raw material, the deterioration processes, and the intervening corrosive agents together with their stability indexes so that it was possible to establish the degradation parameters that these masterpieces had endured.

The results obtained in this pioneering project are presented in this carefully edited book and represent a significant breakthrough in the field of the analysis of the tapestries' physical composition, and in the assessment and transmission of conservation procedures. The beneficiaries are not only the historic European collections from England, Spain and Belgium studied in MODHT, but all tapestries of a similar historic trajectory, including those in the Austrian, French, Polish and Vatican collections, which represent the vast textile heritage so closely related to literature, painting, religious beliefs, court etiquette, and events that have taken place in Europe over the past seven hundred years.

President
PATRIMONIO NACIONAL
April 2009

Introduction

David Howell

TAPESTRIES woven in renowned European centres during the 15th-18th centuries are among the most valuable testimonies of European cultural heritage. When they were first made, they were expensive to produce and used as extremely important emblems of status. Despite tapestries going through stages of being either in or out of fashion, they are now very highly regarded and valued. Their presence in palaces, stately homes, public buildings, churches and cathedrals is an important part of a building's spirit or soul. Their survival, however, is jeopardised by the degradation processes operating in the coloured fibres and metal threads from which they are made.

The maintenance of tapestry collections is not a trivial task. It requires skilled, trained staff, time, space and money. Textile collections need more attention possibly than almost any other type of 'art'. For this reason it is imperative that any owner or other custodian is aware of their responsibilities and has the tools to make the best use of the available resources in this complex process of care.

Tapestries have been repaired almost from the time that they were first made. When new, and used as status symbols, they were subjected to frequent movement. For instance, it is known that at Hampton Court Palace in the 16th century the tapestries were put up or taken down regularly depending on the status of visitors to the palace, and the 2000 or more tapestries then in the collection were far in excess of the area of the walls they were designed to cover. It is also known that tapestries were transported from one palace to another as part of the royal entourage.

Tapestry conservation is a profession that has developed over a relatively short period, having been preceded by the longer tradition of tapestry restoration. Restoration involves removing the original but damaged material and replacing it with modern material. This 'restores' objects to their original appearance and strength but, if repeated many times, will result in an artwork where none of the original tapestry would remain.

Conservation is a much more sympathetic technique where every effort is made to maintain as much historical material as possible with minimal intervention. This will involve not only treatments to remedy damage, but also strategies and actions to prevent damage in the first place, collectively known as preventive conservation.

To understand the problems of tapestry preservation, one needs some knowledge of the structure of the fabric. The *Oxford English Dictionary* defines tapestry as a decorated fabric with a weft containing ornamental designs in coloured wool or silk, gold or silver thread. The important aspect here is that the design is in the base fabric, not applied afterwards as in embroidery or needlepoint. Thus the picture or design is inherent in the textile's structure, rather than a design being applied to a substrate. It is important also to note that while most tapestries are made from wool, many also contain silk. These fibres are both animal materials composed of proteins.

This has major implications for the care, display, storage and repair of tapestries. The important characteristic of tapestries is that in order to display them as intended, they are hung vertically against a wall, quite often suspended solely from the top edge. Depending on how the tapestry is supported at the top, this can result in either a uniform, fairly low tension, or localised higher tensions in the tapestry. Even though the tensions are quite low compared to the initial strength of a tapestry when first made (see chapter 3), it is important to remember that a tapestry must be capable of supporting its own weight.

When in storage the tapestry does not need to be vertical and in most cases tapestries are rolled onto long cylindrical pipes where the tensions are minimal. In storage it is most important to protect the tapestries against insect infestation, high or low relative humidity, high temperature, light and physical forces. But one should not be complacent in thinking that storing them in 'ideal' conditions is enough to preserve these objects, as the results in chapter 4 indicate that even tapestries that have been well looked after in this way may still be in a poor condition many hundreds of years after their manufacture.

Similar preventive measures can be taken to protect tapestries when they are on display. Light levels can be controlled, ultraviolet (UV) light eliminated by use of UV-absorbing window films, the temperature moderated by turning down radiators, and regular inspections made for insect infestation. The objects can be protected from being touched by the public, strategies can be put in place to reduce dust levels and thus minimise potentially damaging cleaning, and in some cases the control of relative humidity is possible through conservation heating, local humidifiers/dehumidifiers, or even air-conditioning systems.

Sometimes curators or conservators are alerted to damage by obvious holes in the tapestry while on display. Often the first areas to open up are slits which were intentionally left in the tapestry as part of the design. These were sewn up by the weaver during production of the tapestry, but because of the nature of the sewing thread (usually linen) and the wider spacing of the threads exerting more tension than the close threads in the main body of the tapestry, these threads tend to degrade first. Quite often the treatment for this is to re-sew the slits and no further action is necessary.

More serious damage to the main fabric of tapestries can be observed by the threads in the weft direction (picks) falling out as they become degraded. The breakdown of the structure of the tapestry itself represents very serious damage which must be treated. This type of damage is sometimes only revealed when a tapestry has to be taken off display for some reason. Moving of the fragile fabric can cause damage which would not have occurred if the tapestry was undisturbed. Further damage may become apparent if the tapestry is wet-cleaned. While conservators can often give quite accurate condition assessments when damage is already occurring, it is more difficult to predict when a tapestry in apparently good condition will start to need interventive conservation treatment.

The principal technique in tapestry conservation has been the sewing of the weakened historical tapestry fabric to new 'support' fabric. There are many opinions as to exact methodologies, but in essence they are all variations on the same theme: making the fabric structure strong enough for the tapestry to be hung without pulling itself apart under its own weight. While the exact nature of treatment varies from country to country and workshop to workshop, there are fairly well agreed criteria for treatment when based on expert examination by trained and experienced staff.

Various degrees of general deterioration can be observed, and some work has been performed on the chemical and physical characterisation of the colorants and on the tapestries themselves. However, there is a great need to be able to ascertain the condition of a tapestry at any specific time, from manufacture when it is at its strongest, to the point where it is actually falling apart. This information is necessary for a number of reasons:

1. Individual collection managers need to be able to prioritise treatments within their collections to be able to estimate resource needs and then allocate that resource expediently.

2. Globally we need to know the general state of our tapestry heritage.

3. Concrete and unequivocal scientific data on specific items can be used to help strengthen the case for funding bids.

There is no question that the final decisions on the treatment of tapestries will be a responsibility shared between curators, collection managers, owners, conservators and any other stakeholders. The need for impartial and scientific data is to allow the discussion between these groups to be as informed as possible in what can be a difficult process. As the MODHT (Monitoring of Damage in Historic Tapestries) project has demonstrated, some preconceptions are seriously, perhaps dangerously, incorrect.

Some results from the MODHT project are the expected scientific data and their interpretation and application to tapestries and tapestry collections. But in addition to this there have been many intangible benefits. The team involved in the research, although all experts in their various fields, became much more conversant with the issues of tapestry conservation as a whole, and have used this knowledge in teaching, public and professional talks, and in publications. The project has had a high profile and brought tapestry conservation to the attention of the heritage profession.

This book captures some of the enthusiasm the project partners have for this work, and the enthusiasm we had for working as an interdisciplinary, multinational team. Hopefully it will inspire enthusiasm in its readers, who can then get involved in the preservation of these remarkable artworks.

TRIUMPH OF DEATH OVER CHASTITY [detail]
(opposite page)

CHAPTER 1
The Approach

CHAPTER 1

The Approach for the MODHT Project

David Howell and Anita Quye

SUCCESSFUL projects of the scale and nature of MODHT rely on careful consideration of the specialist knowledge needed. For the MODHT (Monitoring of Damage in Historic Tapestries) project, seven European partner organisations and their associates were invited to take part, bringing together 24 researchers and practitioners with internationally-recognised expertise in conservation science, textile technology, chemistry, physics, history and conservation (see box on page 11). Good working relationships between the people involved are also essential for fruitful research, and the lead researchers of the partner groups had worked with one another for several years on other projects.

The idea of being able to assess scientifically the condition of historic textiles – and use this assessment to devise novel conservation treatments – had long been an ambition of the project co-ordinator, David Howell. While working with textile curators, he became interested in researching silk degradation. He had developed a particular interest in the degradation of silk (particularly in costume and tapestries) and metal thread cleaning methods. His experience over 20 years had been built up by working on historic textiles with textile conservators, handling both sound and degraded tapestries, undertaking dye analyses, and carrying out tensile strength tests to become familiar with how tapestry weave behaves and how this behaviour changes with age.

The essential factors in putting together the research project were to involve people who were expert in various specific aspects of the project and to define questions that were of practical importance to conservators. Each expert partner had their own perspective and contribution to make. The questions evolved from good communication between the many disciplines involved in the team: conservators who wanted answers to questions such as 'will this tapestry fall apart when I take it off the wall?' and 'how long can this tapestry hang where it is before it will need conservation support?';

curators who wanted their collections to be shown to their best advantage without undue damage, and to be able to plan exhibitions and rotation of exhibits; and scientists who wanted to learn more of the chemistry, physics and mechanics of tapestry and tapestry conservation.

The collective team of scientists had access to a wide range of techniques and expertise to be used in the project. Some research tools were extremely costly and could only be seen as university-level rather than day-to-day techniques affordable by museums and heritage sites. Often the costly techniques provided an enhanced depth of information, which could then be correlated to the results obtained from more widely available techniques.

To make the project feasible within the three-year timescale, it was important to define closely the investigative 'work packages'. There were three main areas to look into:

Investigation 1: The loss of strength with ageing

Tapestries are designed for hanging and require a degree of structural integrity to support their own considerable weight. They are extremely variable in their weave density and condition and so, from a scientific point of view, it was difficult to know how best to choose a representative set of samples. This was a question of interest to all parties and provided perhaps the most interesting and useful information. Because of this, and also because of the ethical issues in ripping apart 'real' objects, it was decided to make replicas (model samples) and to artificially age them for experimentation.

As it is known that light is particularly

FIGURE 1.1 (pages 6 to 7, and opposite)

Some of the MODHT partners examining a tapestry in Brussels in preparation for sampling. (© MODHT Project)

damaging to textiles, especially silk, it was decided that the model samples would be artificially aged by light rather than heat. Artificial ageing has significant disadvantages for experimental research as it can be very difficult to produce accelerated damage regimes which are identical to the mechanisms occurring over much longer timescale in 'natural' or real-life ageing. All of the strength testing (which required large sample sizes) was necessarily carried out on the models, but it was decided that all other viable analytical methods (which required much smaller samples) would be used on both the model and historic samples. This would provide an indirect correlation of the scientific result with the physical state of the historic tapestries.

By understanding the mechanisms of decay, actions can be taken to prevent or slow down further loss; and strategies can be formulated in a systematic and informed way.

Investigation 2: The effect of the different dyes and mordants on fibre strength

This was slightly more complex, but again of great interest to all. Could one predict the likely condition of the tapestry structure by simply knowing which dyes had been used? Or even by which colours had been chosen – does red wool generally degrade more easily than yellow, for example?

Investigation 3: The corrosion of shiny silver and gold threads

From an aesthetic perspective, the metal threads are dulled through tarnishing and become less attractive with age, but it was also essential to assess the effect of the corrosion products on adjoining fibres.

The research 'work packages' discussed above cover every aspect that could be properly researched within the timespan allowed. Certain topics could be omitted because sufficient research had already been carried out in these areas, e.g. the behaviour of red and blue dyes in the presence of light, or the effect of different relative humidities on fading rates and degradation.

Having successfully secured approximately 1.3 million Euros of external funding from the European Commission, the project was initiated. The team began the task of converting a written work plan into an active, multi-partner, pan-European research project. Regular meetings were held at which the team enjoyed open discussions about the interim results, what was important and what was not, which techniques were promising and which ones should be dropped. Nearly all of the meetings included sampling of historic tapestries. This was carried out by the whole group as a team and helped to increase the team's knowledge of tapestries and how to handle them. It was considered very important for the complete research team to be involved in this activity so that different observations could be made by the scientists, conservators and curators during the process.

From these meetings came various protocols to ensure that operations were carried out in the right order, and that the precious samples were circulated in order to maximise the information they could give. Month by month, the number of samples and analytical results increased, and it was important to have a database into which each person could input data. This and the interpretation of the results were perhaps the most important and challenging parts of the project. With so much data it was difficult in some cases to untangle enough to see correlations and draw conclusions. Because the research dealt with so many variables (different dyes, mordants, silk and wool, metals, etc.) and many different scientific approaches and methods, a sub-group was formed to examine the growing database in detail, to ensure that the interpretation was as comprehensive as possible.

After three years the project was complete. This book is a record of the activity over that time and records our conclusions. The ultimate success of the project can only be measured if our results, discussions and conclusion alter the way we think about tapestries and their conservation, and ultimately how we carry out the process of tapestry conservation.

Some of the techniques described here are potentially very powerful tools for conservators and conservation scientists to assess condition by only taking tiny samples from the tapestries, which can then be further utilised for providing other information, such as dye analysis, testing for fugitive dyes in wet-cleaning preparation, and so on. These tools could be invaluable for condition surveys, evaluating tapestries for suitability for wet-cleaning, informing risk assessments for hanging and taking down tapestries, and helping to develop the best systems for tapestry support. It should be said that these techniques will never take the place of experienced skilled conservators, but rather, arm them with additional information to endorse their assessments with objective data.

The conclusions of this research project indicate that tapestries of a certain age are inevitably in an advanced state of degradation, to a certain extent regardless of their storage and display history. This has implications for the urgency to conserve these objects, as well as questioning the reliance we put on preventive measures for preserving historic tapestries.

Partners for MODHT	
1.	Historic Royal Palaces (HRP), United Kingdom
2.	Crown Heritage (Patrimonio Nacional, PNM), Spain
3.	Royal Institute for Cultural Heritage (KIK), Belgium
4.	Birkbeck College, University of London (BbK), United Kingdom
5.	National Museums Scotland (NMS), United Kingdom
6.	University of Manchester, formerly UMIST (UoM), United Kingdom
7.	University of Edinburgh (UoE), United Kingdom

Historic Royal PALACES

PATRIMONIO NACIONAL

1. Historic Royal (HRP), United Kingdom

The MODHT project originated from questions raised by the HRP conservators and conservation scientists about damage assessment for tapestries in the UK Royal Collection, particularly the world famous collection commissioned by Henry VIII in the sixteenth century for Hampton Court Palace, which is owned by the Royal Collection and under the guardianship of HRP. The project was conceived, then led and co-ordinated for the first two years, by David Howell, former Head of Conservation Science, who, with researcher Kathryn Hallett, brought to the project extensive scientific expertise for sampling, fibre analysis (especially silk degradation), tensile strength testing for fabrics, and methods of artificially ageing textiles. Invaluable and unique knowledge of each tapestry's condition, restoration and display record was provided by Lynsay Shephard and her conservation team, complementing the extensive historical perspective from renowned historian Thomas P. Campbell who helped to select the tapestries.

2. Crown Heritage (Patrimonio Nacional, PNM), Spain

Tapestries in the Royal Palace, Madrid, have many parallels with the HRP collections in Hampton Court Palace. Following a fire at Hampton Court Palace in 1986, close relationships between the conservator-restorers from the two institutions developed while establishing how the Belgian tapestries of the 'Story of Tobias' manufactured by Franz Raes had been restored and displayed. PNM art historian Concha Herrero Carretero, a textile specialist with extensive knowledge of the

Spanish Royal Collection, was instrumental in selecting tapestries from the Royal Palace in Madrid for sampling and providing conservation and collection history from documentary sources, assisted by her colleague Ángel Balao González, head of tapestry conservation.

3. Royal Institute for Cultural Heritage (KIK), Belgium

The KIK in Brussels is renowned for its expertise in materials analysis of cultural heritage objects, especially the pioneering work of chemist Jan Wouters, who established liquid chromatography with photodiode array detection for natural dye identification in historical textiles, now used by the world's leading museums. His experience with dyes identified in European tapestries and other textiles was necessary to ensure the model tapestries were dyed with appropriate, authentic dyestuffs. Besides dye analysis, which included non-destructive screening by 3D fluorescence spectrometry, KIK's analytical researchers – Ina Vanden Berghe, Karijn Lamens and Johan Denis – brought to MODHT an emerging successful chromatographic method for protein analysis (developed for historical leather through another European project), along with a newly-developed 3D microscope for examining the metal threads in cross-section. MODHT was further strengthened by Vera Vereecken, one of KIK's textile conservator-restorers, and Ingrid de Meûter, an art historian and curator at Belgium's Royal Museum for Art and History with expertise in Flemish tapestries and the Belgian collections, who selected the tapestries and then arranged access to the collection and their conservation records.

4. Birkbeck College, University of London (BbK), United Kingdom

Thermal analysis of wool and silk fibres is a research specialism of Marianne Odlyha, a scientist at Birkbeck College, experienced in leading and participating in European cultural heritage projects. The novel application of micro thermomechanical analysis and development of non-destructive Fourier transform infrared spectroscopy (FTIR) to measure age-induced changes to fibres by Dr Odlyha and her researchers, Quanyu Wang and Charis Theodorakopoulos, were essential for MODHT. Other methods of fibre analysis for MODHT, including X-ray diffraction, were explored by BbK in collaboration with the UK universities of Cardiff and Exeter.

5. National Museums Scotland (NMS), United Kingdom

Identifying natural dyes in historical textiles by liquid chromatography with photodiode array is a specialism of NMS's analytical chemist, Anita Quye. Her knowledge of natural dyes from analysing NMS's large European textile collection was important for sourcing and checking the dyes for MODHT's models, and her extensive experience from successful collaborations with curators, conservators and academic scientists guided MODHT in sharing the outcomes at a meaningful, practical level for custodians of cultural collections. From her early research of the fading of yellow natural dyes on their analytical result, a close long-term research partnership was formed with the University of Edinburgh (see below), and taken forward in MODHT by their shared PhD researcher, David Peggie.

6. University of Manchester, formerly UMIST (UoM), United Kingdom

The internationally-recognised expertise in textile chemistry, manufacturing and processing methods, and surface analysis at UoM was brought to MODHT by Chris Carr and PhD researcher Marei Hacke. Without the university's facilities, machinery and industrial experience, the challenging and time-intensive task of dyeing and weaving the model tapestries would not have been possible. Production of the model tapestries was vital for giving the project an objective scientific foundation for interpreting the historical tapestries' results. UoM also sourced the metal threads and undertook the corrosion experiments on them. Specialised administrative skills and experience are important for European-funded projects to ensure correct reporting and financial procedures, and this was provided by Gwynfor Hughes at UoM, with Chris Carr co-ordinating the final third year of MODHT.

7. University of Edinburgh (UoE), United Kingdom

The extensive and complementary organic chemistry knowledge of Alison Hulme and Hamish McNab, both lecturers at UoE provided essential understanding for the light-induced degradation of the yellow and redwood dyes investigated by David Peggie, the PhD researcher working collaboratively with NMS (see above). The excellent cutting-edge analytical facilities at the UoE coupled with collaborative research with NMS had already established tandem mass spectrometry as an important analytical tool for historical dye analysis. This was applied and developed further in MODHT, along with nuclear magnetic resonance spectroscopy, to understand the chemically complex redwood dyes.

FIGURE 1.2

The MODHT team gathered at Bruges to study three tapestries and take samples for analysis.
(© MODHT Project)

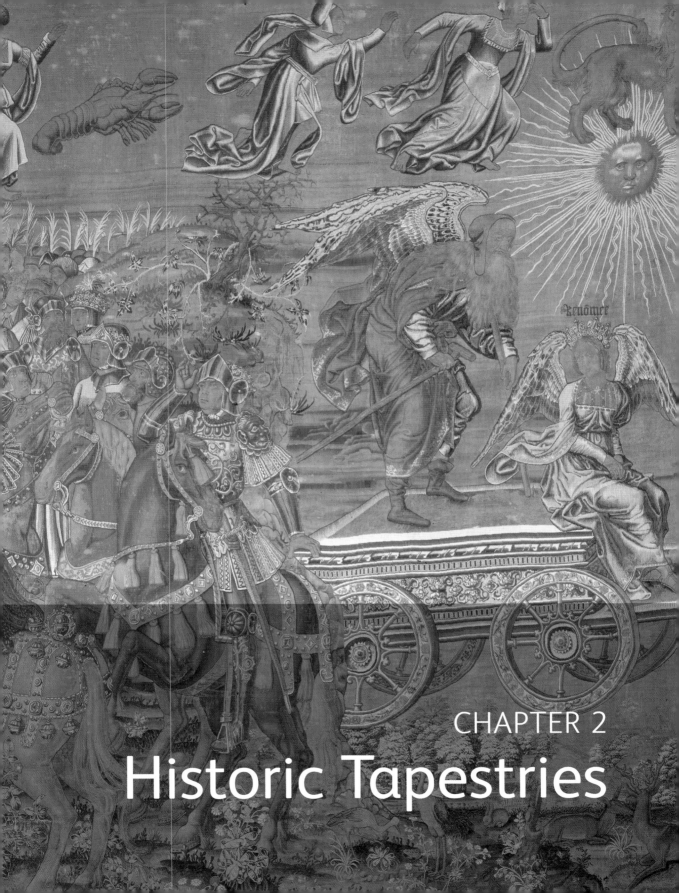

CHAPTER 2
Historic Tapestries

CHAPTER 2

Historic Tapestries

Concha Herrero Carretero
(translated by Ines Castellano-Colmenero)

THE MODHT project focused on three important European historic tapestry collections from Spain, England and Belgium. This chapter describes the historical significance and background of each collection, as far as they are known.

Recent research has confirmed, once again, the great value and finery of tapestries in royal, ecclesiastical and aristocratic collections; it has also documented their use as rich and magnificent objects for furnishing.[1,2] Most significantly, it has revealed the true character of tapestries as works of art and carriers of deep symbolic and allegorical meaning. However, little systematic research has been done on their physical characteristics.

Courtly by nature, tapestries were from the outset symbols of the power, rank and grandeur of the proprietor or exhibitor. Besides bestowing their unquestionable thermal properties as a traditional decorative furnishing, especially for royal residences, their excellent imagery and iconography have proved exceptionally useful as propaganda tools. A tapestry is a polychromatic fabric reproducing a cartoon by means of the regular interweaving of a blend of filamentous fibres of silk or wool, and often of silver and gold, to obtain a great variety of composition effects. Tapestry, like painting, is not only a decorative art, but also a narrative one, capable of representation, storytelling and portrayal of individuals or landscapes. These characteristics made tapestries important conveyors of religious and political symbols.

From Medieval times, the distinguished decorative role of tapestries as official art has included many important events of public life: liturgical and courtly ceremonies have seen them used in coronations, banquets, processions, tournaments, canonizations, baptisms and royal weddings. Being portable and relatively easy to spatially rearrange, they have adorned interiors and exteriors, and have also been used to form silk chambers. Therefore, they have long been essential items in ceremonies and celebrations, even to the present day (see Figure 2.2).

Rich iconography is an intrinsic characteristic of tapestries. Through the ages, secular and religious themes have been taken to the looms and transferred to colourful hangings. Important religious cycles that relate the life and passion of Christ, episodes from the Bible, devout or moralizing stories, narrations from the popular or chivalrous literature of the time, classical and mythological adaptations, everyday life, country or hunting scenes have adorned interior chambers and urban spaces.

Tapestries have always had a clear architectural basis: as a set of panels intended to cover the walls of a room or an exterior space, cloisters, façades or balconies. 'To hang with tapestries' was therefore the action of attaching the tapestries on to a wall to furnish and dress a room or a façade, with suspension cords attached to the upper linen part from which to hang it.

Art and technique: tapestry-making

Tapestry-making was a labour-intensive, highly skilled and long process, with highest quality production sometimes taking years to complete. The tapestries were manually woven on special looms, either vertical (high-warp tapestry) or horizontal (low-warp tapestry); a plain weave is normally used (also known as tabby or taffeta weave). The technique, the execution of the fabric and the resulting textile are identical whether the piece has been woven on a high or a low warp loom. Once the tapestry has been finished, cut and taken

FIGURE 2.1 (pages 14 to 15, and opposite)

Details of *Triumph of Time over Fame* tapestry, 'Triumph of Petrarch' series, Hampton Court Palace. (The Royal Collection © 2009 Her Majesty Queen Elizabeth II)

FIGURE 2.2 (above)

At the 2004 Spanish Royal Wedding of Prince Felipe, the Cathedral was hung with tapestries, continuing the traditional use of these textiles to embellish significant court events. (© Patrimonio Nacional)

off the loom, it is thus impossible to determine on what type of loom it was woven unless there is documentation available.

The system of interweaving the threads is simple in tapestries, consisting of the alternate interlacing of two set of threads that cross each other at right angles. One set is the warp and follows the longitudinal direction of the textile, and the other is the weft which follows the transverse direction of the fabric. This is the so-called plain (or tabby, or taffeta) weave where the weft threads go alternatively over and under the warp threads, which are always stronger and more twisted than the weft threads. In this kind of textile, the multicoloured weft threads form the patterns by following the chosen design – they totally cover the undyed threads of the warp when interlacing. This is why the tapestry is referred to as 'weft faced', since the weft, when pushed down in the loom by the combs, completely covers the warp which can only be discerned by the characteristic ridged surface of the tapestry.

The nature of tapestry production meant that warps created a series of ridges on the textile's surface. This casts unwelcome shadows, so light-reflecting threads were incorporated to counteract the darkening effect. Shiny threads of precious metal, typically gold, silver and gilded silver, were the inevitable expensive option. Although popular in the 16th century, their high price meant that use declined from the 17th century until abandoned in most weaving centres by the 18th century. An effective alternative was silk dyed in light tones, particularly yellow, which imparted striking luminosity and richness that evoked the qualities of a precious material. Unfortunately these dyes were prone to fading, resulting in the loss of this glorious effect in many of today's historical tapestries.

From the 14th to 18th centuries, European

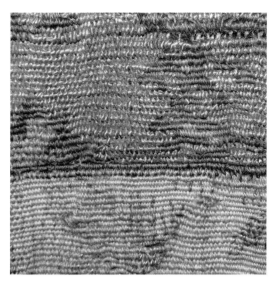

FIGURE 2.3

Dovetail technique for changing the colour of yarn in the weft direction. (© Historic Royal Palaces)

manufacturers shared three common characteristic techniques for permitting a change of the coloured yarn being used during tapestry weaving: dovetail, slit and interlock.

1. *Dovetailing* involved weaving dyed wefts in a zig-zag fashion so that the different coloured yarns appear interlaced as they turn over a common warp [Fig. 2.3]. This imparted a distinctive visual appearance of blended colour not dissimilar to that of a painting, so was aesthetically the best of all three methods. The staggered nature of the interfaces (also known as *hachures*) kept the internal structure intact, making dovetailed tapestries relatively strong.

2. The *slit* method compromised the strength of a tapestry the most, although it was the quickest form of tapestry making. When coloured yarns were changed by looping the ends of weft threads back around the same warp, the interlacing action of the weft was interrupted and

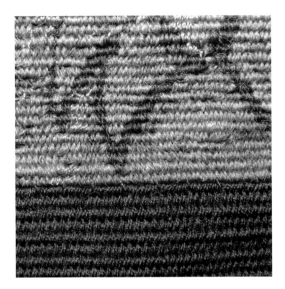

FIGURE 2.4

Slit technique for changing the colour of yarn in the weft direction. (© Historic Royal Palaces)

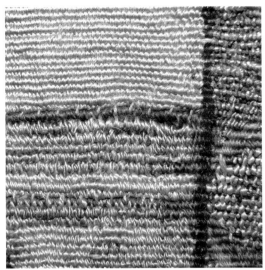

FIGURE 2.5

Interlock technique for changing the colour of yarn in the weft direction. (© Historic Royal Palaces)

formed a slit if repeated more than three times consecutively. When weaving was completed, selvedges were sewn together with back-stitch using a needle [see Fig. 2.4]. This technique was mainly used to join areas representing the sky or the ground to the figurative parts, so slit joins are common at the top and bottom of tapestries. They are also often found at the top of an inferior selvedge where separate strips of single colour run parallel to the warp to frame the tapestry. Selvedges were used by manufacturers and weavers to weave in their maker's marks, which became obligatory from the 16th century. Slits invariably become weak points in the tapestry because of the lack of cohesion between weft and warp. Thus, over time, these fragile seams have been frequently damaged by rubbing or tearing due to the weight of the tapestries. Many pieces have now lost their original selvedges, along with reference to both their manufacturer and weavers.

3. The third weaving method is to interlace weft threads on the reverse side when changing coloured yarns, called *interlocking* [Fig. 2.5]. This technique avoided creating slits, and consequently needle-sewn seams were unnecessary. Although a lot more time and work was invested for interlocked weaving, the payback was a much stronger tapestry with a better unified structure. Interlock weave tapestries therefore tend to be more resilient to wear and tear, and able to bear their own weight better than those made with the other two weaving methods.

The fragility of tapestries explains the loss of large numbers of pieces due to use and progressive ageing of the fibres, although the major losses have been due to human factors such as fire, war and a lack of understanding of the effects of neglect and mistreatment.

The historic tapestry collections in the project

A strong partnership between significant and related European collections was fundamental in giving the MODHT research valued meaning. On this front, the project was exceptionally fortunate to have involved Spain's Crown Heritage (Patrimonio Nacional), the United Kingdom's Historic Royal Palaces, the Belgian Royal Museum of Art and History, Brussels, and the Belgian cities of Bruges and Tournai.

The Spanish and the United Kingdom partner institutions between them care for two of the most valuable and substantial European historic collections assembled during the 16th and 17th centuries. In the Palacio Real, Madrid are the collections assembled by the House of Habsburg or House of Austria in Spain; while Hampton Court Palace, near London, maintains a collection assembled by English monarchs, an especially important set being that of Henry VIII (1509-47). These two royal collections have many parallels regarding their assemblage, content and conservation.

Complementing these collections were tapestries selected from four prestigious Belgian collections. Those in the Royal Museum's collection were assembled at the end of the 19th century by Leopold II, who followed a systematic acquisition of well-known works by Flemish manufacturers. Cultural protection exercised over the Belgian historic and artistic collection has meant the assemblages in the cathedral of Notre-Dame of Tournai, in the Musées Communaux and in the Musée Notre-Dame de la Poterie in Bruges have been retained there since manufacture.

The first priority for the project was deciding which tapestries to study, and this was agreed at the inaugural meeting, held in Madrid in October 2002 at the Palacio Real. Seventeen tapestries across the partner collections were selected by Concha Herrero Carretero, Ingrid de Meûter and Tom Campbell, representing tapestries from the 15th to the 17th centuries produced by the great manufacturing centres of Arras, Brussels, Bruges and Antwerp. At the same meeting, protocols for sampling, cataloguing and sample distribution between the analytical partners were approved (see chapter 5 and appendix 2), which enabled the sampling of the Palacio Real's collections to commence.

The second sampling workshop, in February 2003, was multi-centred and involved Tournai Cathedral, the Musées Communaux in Bruges, the Musée Notre-Dame de la Poterie in Bruges and the Royal Museum of Art and History of Brussels. The third and final sampling workshop was for the UK Royal Collection at Hampton Court Palace in September 2003. The effort of arranging access to unroll more than 85 metres of priceless and delicate, yet heavy, tapestries, then making multi-disciplinary decisions on areas to study, and maintaining the physical and mental stamina to consistently and meticulously sample and record 586 yarns and metallic threads, was intense. That this all took a combined total of just six working days was a satisfying achievement and testament to the enormous amount of preparation, co-ordination, team effort and respect between the participating institutions and project partners.

The objective of the three sampling campaigns was to obtain samples of metallic threads, wool and silk fibres from the back and, in a few exceptional cases, from the front, in order to carry out microscopic, physical and chemical analysis. The aim was to evaluate the composition of the fibres and to identify chemical markers of damage to assess the degradation of fibres and dyestuffs caused by exposure to light and changes in atmospheric conditions. This was the first time that any historical tapestry had been subjected to such systematic research to understand its condition. For the chosen few in the project, the legacy of expert multi-disciplinary attention will benefit them in many ways in their public enjoyment and understanding for years to come.

NOTE: *The following pages (22-38) contain information about all the tapestries selected for the MODHT project. Please note that colour variation between tapestry images reproduced in this book is due to photography having taken place at different times and in various locations. The colours are therefore not necessarily accurate for each tapestry or its details.*

FIGURES 2.6 and 2.7

Hampton Court Palace, London (above) and Palacio Real, Madrid (below), home to some of Europe's finest tapestries. (Figs. 2.6 © Historic Royal Palaces and 2.7 © Kathryn Hallett)

MODHT code: PNM1

Location of sampling: PRM

Title of Tapestry: *Daedalus and Icarus*

Series: Fables of Ovid

Registration no: PN.10026390

Date: 1545

Location of manufacture:
Brussels, Willem de Pannemaker
(active 1535-81)

Materials: wool, silk, metal thread

Dyes identified through analysis:
dyer's greenweed, indigoid, madder, weld,
brazilwood, young fustic (metal thread core)

Weave count: 9-9.5 warp per cm

Size (cm): 357 x 518

Images © Patrimonio Nacional

PRM = Palacio Real, Madrid

MODHT code: PNM2

Location of sampling: PRM

Title of Tapestry: *Jupiter and Ganymede*

Series: Fables of Ovid

Registration no: PN.10026392

Date: 1545

Location of manufacture: Brussels, Willem de Pannemaker (active 1535-81)

Materials: wool, silk, metal thread

Dyes identified through analysis: dyer's greenweed, indigoid, weld, madder, brazilwood, Mexican cochineal, young fustic (metal thread core)

Weave count: 9-9.5 warp per cm

Size (cm): 355 x 339

Images © Patrimonio Nacional

PRM = Palacio Real, Madrid

MODHT code: PNM5

Location of sampling: PRM

Title of Tapestry: *Neoptolemus and Polyxena*

Series: Fables of Ovid

Registration no: PN.10004159

Date: 1545

Location of manufacture:
Brussels, Willem de Pannemaker
(active 1535-81)

Materials: wool, silk, metal thread

Dyes identified through analysis:
weld, madder, indigoid, brazilwood, dyer's
greenweed, young fustic (metal thread core)

Weave count: 9-9.5 warp per cm

Size (cm): 355 x 587

Images © Patrimonio Nacional (and opposite page)

PRM = Palacio Real, Madrid

MODHT code: PNM7

Location of sampling: PRM

Title of Tapestry: *Tobias presents Raphael to his Father*

Series: Story of Tobias

Registration no: PN.10004043

Date: 1550

Location of manufacture:
Brussels, Balthazar van Vlierden
(active 1547)

Materials: wool, silk

Dyes identified through analysis:
weld, indigoid, dyer's greenweed,
madder

Weave count: 8-8.5 warp per cm

Size (cm): 454 x 665

PRM = Palacio Real, Madrid

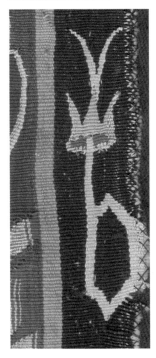

MODHT code: PNM8

Location of sampling: PRM

Title of Tapestry: *Atalanta hunts the Calydonian Wild Boar*

Series: Story of Diana

Registration no: PN.10004073

Date: 1620

Location of manufacture: Bruges

Materials: wool, silk

Dyes identified through analysis: madder, weld, indigoid

Weave count: 7-7.5 warp per cm

Size (cm): 410 x 462

Images © Patrimonio Nacional

PRM = Palacio Real, Madrid

MODHT code: PNM9

Location of sampling: PRM

Title of Tapestry: *Wine Arbours Gallery*

Series: Galleries

Registration no: PN.10004350

Date: 1660

Location of manufacture:
Antwerp, Jacob Wauters
(active 1619-60)

Materials: wool, silk

Dyes identified through analysis:
weld, brazilwood, munjeet

Weave count: 6-7 warp per cm

Size (cm): 132 x 163

Images © Patrimonio Nacional

PRM = Palacio Real, Madrid

MODHT code: TOU1

Location of sampling: TC

Title of Tapestry: *Life of Saint Piat*

Series: Story of Saint Piat and Saint Eleuthere

Registration no: −

Date: 1402

Location of manufacture:
    Arras, Pierrot Feré

Materials: wool

Dyes identified through analysis:
    madder, indigoid, weld, unidentified
    synthetic

Weave count: 7 warp per cm

Size (cm): 186 x 282

Images © Ingrid de Meûter

TC = Tournai Cathedral

MODHT code: BRU1

Location of sampling: BMC

Title of Tapestry: *Verdure with Coat of Arms of Brugse Vrije* (fragments)

Series: 15 tapestries made for the Brugse Vrije

Registration no: Inv. O.1.XVII

Date: 1530

Location of manufacture: Bruges

Materials: wool

Dyes identified through analysis: dyer's greenweed, indigoid, weld, madder, tannin

Weave count: 4-5 warp per cm

Size (cm): 86 x 148 (largest fragment)

© 2009 Museum Bruges – images courtesy of Reproductiefonds

BMC = Bruges Musées Communaux

MODHT code: BRU2

Location of sampling: BMNDP

Title of Tapestry: *Mary's Presentation in the Temple*

Series: Life of the Virgin

Registration no: Inv. O.P.1007.XV11

Date: 1639

Location of manufacture: Bruges

Materials: wool

Dyes identified through analysis: weld, madder, indigoid, Mexican cochineal

Weave count: 5-6 warp per cm

Size (cm): 370 x 422.5

BMNDP = Bruges Musée Notre-Dame de la Poterie

MODHT code: BRU3

Location of sampling: BMNDP

Title of Tapestry: One from 'Miracles of Our Lady of the Poterie' series

Series: Miracles of Our Lady of the Poterie

Registration no: Inv. O.P.160b XV11

BMNDP = Bruges Musée Notre-Dame de la Poterie

Date: 1630

Location of manufacture: Bruges

Materials: wool

Dyes identified through analysis: madder, weld, indigoid, synthetic indigo

Weave count: 5 warp per cm

Size (cm): 173.5 x 532.5

MODHT code: BXL1

Location of sampling: RMAH

Title of Tapestry: *Justice disarmed by Mercy*

Series: The Triumphs of the Virtues over the Vices

Registration no: Inv. 9923

Date: 1519-24

Location of manufacture: Brussels

Materials: wool, silk

Dyes identified through analysis: dyer's greenweed, indigoid, madder, weld

Weave count: 6-7 warp per cm

Size (cm): 413 x 652

RMAH = Royal Museum of Art and History, Brussels

MODHT code: BXL2

Location of sampling: RMAH

Title of Tapestry: *Christ before Pilate*

Series: Set of 4 Passion tapestries

Registration no: Inv. 9739

Date: 1520

Location of manufacture: Brussels

Materials: wool, silk, metal thread

Dyes identified through analysis:
madder, old fustic, logwood, tannin,
weld, Mexican cochineal, young fustic
(metal thread core)

Weave count: 8 warp per cm

Size (cm): 300 x 380

Images © Royal Museum of Art and History /
Musées Royaux d'Art et d'Histoire

RMAH = Royal Museum of Art and History, Brussels

MODHT code: BXL3

Location of sampling: RMAH

Title of Tapestry: *The Legend of Herkenbald*

Series: unique piece

Registration no: Inv. 865

Date: 1513

Location of manufacture:
    Brussels, Lyon de Smedt

Materials: wool, silk, metal thread

Dyes identified through analysis:
    dyer's greenweed, brazilwood, munjeet,
    indigoid, madder

Weave count: 7 warp per cm

Size (cm): 387 x 430

RMAH = Royal Museum of Art and History, Brussels

MODHT code: BXL4

Location of sampling: RMAH

Title of Tapestry: *Man and the Seven Deadly Sins*

Series: The Triumphs of the Virtues over the Vices

Registration no: Inv. 9921

Date: 1519-24

Location of manufacture: Brussels

Materials: wool, silk

Dyes identified through analysis: madder, dyer's greenweed, weld, indigoid, young fustic (metal thread core)

Weave count: 6-7 warp per cm

Size (cm): 411 x 650

Images © Musées Royaux d'Art et d'Histoire

RMAH = Royal Museum of Art and History, Brussels

MODHT code: HRP1

Location of sampling: HCP

Title of Tapestry: *Triumph of Time over Fame*

Series: Triumphs of Petrarch

Registration no: RC1270.3

Date: *c*.1515

Location of manufacture: Brussels

Materials: wool, silk

Dyes identified through analysis: indigoid, weld, dyer's greenweed, logwood, purpurin, madder, lichen, unidentified synthetic

Weave count: 7-8 warp per cm

Size (cm): 355 x 587

HCP = Hampton Court Palace, United Kingdom

MODHT code: HRP2

Location of sampling: HCP

Title of Tapestry: *Tobias presents Raphael to his Father*

Series: Story of Tobias

Registration no: RC1364

Date: *c.*1544/46

Location of manufacture: Brussels

Materials: wool, silk, metal thread

Dyes identified through analysis: Mexican cochineal, indigoid, dyer's greenweed, tannin, old fustic, ellagic acid, weld, madder, brazil-wood, lichen, young fustic (metal thread core)

Weave count: 7-8 warp per cm

Size (cm): 450 x 672

Image: The Royal Collection © 2009 Her Majesty Queen Elizabeth II

HCP = Hampton Court Palace, United Kingdom

MODHT code: HRP3

Location of sampling: HCP

Title of Tapestry: *Triumph of Death over Chastity*

Series: Triumphs of Petrarch

Registration no: RC1270.4

Date: *c.*1515

Location of manufacture: Brussels

Materials: wool, silk

Dyes identified through analysis: madder, weld, dyer's greenweed, indigoid, Weave count: 7-8 warp per cm

Size (cm): 403 x 823

Images: The Royal Collection © 2009 Her Majesty Queen Elizabeth II

HCP = Hampton Court Palace, United Kingdom

The history of the collections

The Spanish Royal Collection

Since the 19th century, the Spanish Royal Collection of tapestries has been considered the most comprehensive in Europe for Flemish production between the 15th and 17th centuries. Containing more than 500 pieces from the main Flemish workshops in Brussels, Bruges and Antwerp, the collection is itself an important reference for the monograms and marks of manufacturers and weavers from four centuries of tapestry-making for the European courts, such as Pieter van Aelst, Willem de Pannemaker, Pieter de Kempeneer, Jan Raes, Jacob Geubels and Jacob Wauters. With over 800 additional tapestries woven in Madrid during the 18th century, the traditional decorative use of tapestry at court and ecclesiastical events continues today for celebrations, significant public processions and royal ceremonies. The tapestries therefore require special care for their preservation.

The Habsburg and Bourbon monarchs who ruled Spain considered their tapestries symbolic of the Crown's authority. Acquisitions made during the reign of Isabella 'the Catholic' of Spain (Isabel 'la Católica') (1451-1504), and especially those of Charles I (Carlos I), Holy Roman Emperor (1500-58), and Philip II (Felipe II) (1527-98), augmented the collection with Flemish masterpieces such as the *Paños de Oro* (*Veneration of the Virgin*), the *Honours*, the *Conquest of Tunis* and the *Apocalypse*.

Successive inheritances and direct requests to the Flemish weavers progressively enriched the royal tapestries. Its assemblage and protection continued, thanks to Philip II who linked the collection to the Crown, thereby

FIGURE 2.8 (see also 2.2)

Tapestries form an impressive backdrop for the Spanish Royal Wedding of Prince Felipe in 2004.
(© Patrimonio Nacional)

providing protection from the sales and auctions which traditionally followed the death of a monarch.

Restoration and conservation of the Spanish Royal Collection

Historically, the care of tapestries in the Spanish Royal Collection was carried out by the Oficio de la Tapicería [Tapestry Office], which was staffed by Flemish master weavers whose duties were to organise, store, clean, line and mend the tapestries to decorate the royal rooms. The position of *retupidor* (tapestry-mender), created in the 15th century, was occupied by Flemish masters who carried out the inevitable work of *encañonado* and *retupido*: repairing the yarns and cleaning the pieces in the Manzanares river during the summer period. Inventories kept by the heads of the office provide invaluable primary sources of information for identifying the tapestries' narrative sequences. Moreover, they offer detailed information about the dimensions of the pieces and the yarn compositions, whether silk, wool or gold and silver metal threads.

Eventually the Royal Tapestry Manufacture at Madrid replaced the Tapestry Office for the restoration and cleaning of the collection and, from 1720, after establishing itself at Santa Bárbara House, it began a close collaboration with master weaver Van der Goten, who arrived from Antwerp.

All through the 16th and up to the 19th century the heads of the Tapestry Office and the Royal Tapestry Manufacture undertook the periodical replacement of the tapestries hung in the Royal chambers following the change in the seasons. Their jobs were also to hang up and take down the sets decorating the chapel and Royal apartments, and arrange the transport of the pieces when the court changed residence. Other duties included the installation of canopies and the ornamentation of the Palace's façades for courtly ceremonies such as the victory parades of princes and kings, or for religious festivals such as Corpus Christi.

Historically the conservation of tapestries consisted of the beating, cleaning, lining and darning of the pieces requiring care. The cleaning process involved dusting, brushing, washing with soap and water in the river, and the drying of the tapestries in the sun.

Present-day conservation workshops are dedicated to preventative care and to the undertaking of reversible intervention when it is required to procure the consolidation of any deteriorated textile structure and to avoid any stress to pieces that are being exhibited. Their aim is to stop any degradation process slowing down

FIGURE 2.9

Textile washing in the Manzanares river, Madrid, late 18th century. (© Patrimonio Nacional)

the ageing of the fibres due to the tensions exercised on the pieces by their weight.

Today's tapestry storage system for the Spanish Royal Collection is the result of a project started in 1987 to substitute the previous unsatisfactory (in modern conservation terms) traditional system of folding tapestries and storing them on shelves. Between 1987 and 1989 the building was developed and appropriate furniture installed before the transfer of more than 2000 pieces to the improved store. The biggest tapestries are now rolled onto cylinders and grouped in compact cupboards, with tapestry fragments stored in trays inside flat drawers.

given in 2000 for the building of a new Museum of the Royal Collection, the design of which has been led by the tapestry collection.

FIGURE 2.10

The European Historic Exhibition in 1892. (© Patrimonio Nacional)

FIGURE 2.11

An official ceremony for Alfonso XIII in 1924. (© Patrimonio Nacional)

FIGURE 2.12

Modern tapestry storage system at the Palacio Real, Madrid, 2002. (© Patrimonio Nacional)

Displaying the Spanish Royal Collection

Since the 19th century there has been a recognised need for a specific museum devoted to displaying the Royal Collection. This has, in recent times, been developed by Patrimonio Nacional in Madrid, whose displays included rooms devoted to tapestry in the palaces of San Ildefonso and El Escorial. Approval was

Fig. 2.10

Fig. 2.11

Fig. 2.12

The English Royal Collection

Tapestry was the pre-eminent art form of the English Tudor court, valued for its beauty, its luxury and, above all, as a dramatic, portable means of demonstrating royal power and ideals. During his reign King Henry VIII amassed an unrivalled collection of tapestries numbering more than 900 pieces, of which the finest were richly woven in gold after designs by the leading artists of the time. Now largely dispersed or destroyed, Henry's extensive inventory reveals how, through tapestry, he identified himself with particular historic, religious and mythological figures, putting England in dialogue and competition with the leading courts of early modern Europe while at the same time promoting his own religious and political agendas at home.[2]

The splendid collection totalled, according to the inventories of the Royal Wardrobe written in 1688,[3] nearly 900 pieces including those previously belonging to Cardinal Wolsey confiscated by Henry VIII, the purchases of the king from 1540, and the pieces woven in Mortlake for Charles I. After Charles' execution, the collection was dispersed, sold or destroyed. For this reason, although still keeping pieces of great artistic value like the *Triumphs of Petrarch* or the biblical stories of *Abraham* or *Tobias* at Hampton Court Palace, it cannot compare in quantity to the Spanish Royal Collection.

As in the Spanish and other royal courts, there was an employee in charge of the care of the tapestries, their cleaning and the repair needed due to the continuous use of the pieces. In the English collection this employee was the Lord Chamberlain, who was responsible

FIGURE 2.13

The tapestry conservation studio at Hampton Court Palace.
(© Historic Royal Palaces)

for the Royal Wardrobe. He had parallel functions to those of the *Tapicero Mayor* (head tapestry curator) of the Spanish Royal Collection, who was responsible for the Royal Tapestry Manufacture. The Lord Chamberlain's duties, among others, were the periodical decoration and furnishing of the royal apartments, using tapestries for the adornment of ceremonies such as royal coronations and the reception of diplomats. He also oversaw the delivery of tapestries to master restorers, who would carry out the regular and necessary duties of lining, cleaning and repair, and whose names – Vanderbank, Vandenborg, Vandergoten – reveal their Flemish origin.

Textile conservation has a long history at Hampton Court Palace. A tapestry restoration workshop was founded in 1912, under the management of Morris & Co., to rectify the deteriorating condition of the tapestries at Hampton Court Palace. By 1979 this had evolved into a cutting-edge modern conservation department and scientific laboratory, treating a wide range of objects. Today it is recognised for its technical skills and scientific expertise in the conservation of large textiles displayed in the context of historic buildings. The Conservation and Collection Care team (CCC) carries out treatments on tapestries, state beds and furnishing textiles, royal and court costume, and has a unique wet-cleaning facility, store and analytical laboratory.

The Royal Museum of Art and History (Musées Royaux d'Art et d'Histoire), Brussels

Complementing the two royal collections described above in terms of assemblage, maintenance and repair, the Belgian collection was, from the beginning, cared for as a collection of museum objects. The current Royal Museum of Art and History in Brussels originated as the Musée du Cinquantenaire. It was built at the end of the 19th century during the reign of Leopold II and briefly renamed the Musée Royaux du Parc du Cinquantenaire between 1912 and 1922. In 1946 part of the museum suffered a devastating fire with part of the collection reduced to ashes. After a lengthy building restoration project, the institution embarked on an ambitious programme to purchase tapestries and also to modernise itself before reopening in 1966.

Today the Royal Museum of Art and History houses the most important collection of tapestries in Belgium, a total of 150 pieces, including those from the workshops of Brussels, Tournai and Oudenaarde. For conservation reasons not all can be on permanent display. Instead a biennially changing exhibition programme allows about 40 different pieces to be shown at any time. They range in styles and artistic trends, from the Middle Ages to the present day, thereby offering a comprehensive perspective of the various weaving production centres.

Centres of manufacture represented in MODHT

This section provides an examination of the historical centres of tapestry manufacture in a geographical and chronological order, with reference made to the tapestries chosen for study during the MODHT project.

Tapestries made in Arras

Patronage by the Burgundian Dukes, Philip the Bold (reign 1363-1404), Philip the Good (1419-67), Charles the Bold (r.1467-77) and Mary of Burgundy (1477-82), during the 14th and 15th centuries, benefited the tapestry industry of Arras, capital city of Artois. Arras production corresponds to the Gothic tapestry period which lasted from the 13th century until the first quarter of the 16th century. Although details in the collections' records used for MODHT indicate a number that could have come out of the Arras workshops, we were only certain of the origin of the set titled 'Story of Saint Piat and Saint Eleuthere', woven in 1402 and kept in the cathedral of Tournai. It was commissioned by Toussaint Pierre, canon of the cathedral and chaplain to Philip the Good. The two panels tell the story of the two patron saints of the cathedral, Piat and Eleuthere, who, around AD 300 in the Merovingian era, christened the city of Tournai and its surroundings. Woven by Pierrot Feré, they were given to the cathedral in December 1402 where they have remained ever since. Today they adorn the walls of the oval chapel of the Holy Ghost. The tapestry analysed from this set was the *Life of Saint Piat* [TOU1].

This tapestry from Tournai is of a type known as 'choir tapestries', woven in the 14th century and donated by the canons to cathedral churches. These tapestries usually tell the story of patron saints, as in the *Life of the Saints Gervasius and Protasius* in the Le Mans Cathedral and the *Life of Saint Stephen* in the Cathedral of Auxerre.[4] It is now assumed that the pieces had a parallel function to that of the *Biblia Pauperum* as a very useful means of instructing devotees through illustrations and text in the popular language, besides reinforcing fraternity among canons.

The production of high warp tapestry in Arras is proven by documents dating from 1313. Arras' weavers settled in Tournai in 1352, bringing their industry to the city. Their statutes of 26 March 1398 are the oldest of this type in existence in the Low Countries.[5] The competition exercised by Tournai from the first half of the 15th century and the siege of the city of Arras by Louis XI in 1477, were the initiators of its decline as a manufacture centre for the production of tapestries.

Tapestries made in Brussels

The Dukes of Burgundy continued their patronage of the weaving centres from 1477 and, after the marriage of Mary of Burgundy with the emperor Maximilian I (Holy Roman Emperor 1508-19), the support was taken up by their siblings, the kings of the House of Habsburg or House of Austria, who became ardent collectors of tapestries. Brussels outshone the rest of the weaving centres and became, from the beginning of the 16th century and most notably from 1526, the major and best quality producer of tapestries of the southern Low Countries.

A crucial point for the dating of the

production of Brussels' tapestries was the imperial edict of 1544 by which all workshops and weavers were to adopt a mark of city and workshop to avoid frauds and to guarantee the quality of the production. Nevertheless, five of the tapestries incorporated into the MODHT project predate the imperial edict and for this reason lack the marks and monograms of manufacturers. These are *The Legend of Herkenbald* [BXL3], two pieces in 'The Triumphs of the Virtues over the Vices' series (*Justice disarmed by Mercy* [BXL1] and *Man and the Seven Deadly Sins* [BXL4]), and two pieces of the 'Triumphs of Petrarch' series (*Triumph of Time over Fame* [HRP1] and *Triumph of Death over Chastity* [HRP3]).

These tapestries keep within the tradition of the previous period, reflecting the increasing influence of German and, particularly, Italian art of the 15th century. They are classed in the pre-Renaissance period of Flemish tapestry, in parallel to the regency of Margaret of Austria over the Low Countries (r.1507-30).

The tapestry *Legend of Herkenbald* [BXL3] was commissioned by the Confrérie du Saint Sacrement of the Church of Saint Pierre at Louvain, in whose chapel it hung in 1513. The panel had a clear doctrinal and liturgical intention, very close to that of the choir tapestries of the previous century. The scene, selected from the *Dialogus miraculorum* of the Cistercian monk Caesarius of Heisterbach (1180-23), tells the story of the Comte Erkenbaldus of Burdan or Herkenbald who, on his deathbed, was refused the sacrament of communion for not repenting the trial and execution of his nephew, who had seduced a lady. The consecrated wafer, nevertheless, alighted on his tongue as divine proof of the fairness of his judgment. The liturgical value of the main scene is underlined by the motifs of the Mystic Lamb, the chalice and the consecrated wafer that appear boxed within the rich flowery wreath. The tapestry belongs to the group of 'retable' tapestries, which are highly characteristic of the early period of tapestry production in

FIGURES 2.14 and 2.15

Monograms of weaver Willem de Pannemaker in *Daedalus and Icarus* [PNM1] (left) and *Jupiter and Ganymede* [PNM2] (right). (Images © Patrimonio Nacional)

FIGURE 2.16

Willem de Pannemaker's monogram in *Neoptolemus and Polyxena* [PMN5]. (© Patrimonio Nacional)

FIGURE 2.17

Monogram of Bruges in *Atlanta hunts the Calydonian wild boar* [PMN8]. (© Patrimonio Nacional)

Brussels. It is attributed to the weaver Lyon de Smedt following the cartoons of Jean van Roome, a painter devoted to the realisation of sketches not only for tapestries, but also for retables and stained glass windows.[6] The tapestry was purchased by the Royal Museum of Art and History in 1862.

The richness and iconographic complexity of tapestries is characteristic of this art form. Typical for this period are the moralistic allegories of vices and virtues born under the influence of the Lutheran iconography and inspired by the plays of the 15th and 16th centuries, which were very much admired in the southern Low Countries. 'The Triumphs of the Virtues over the Vices' series, woven between 1519 and 1524, was an important donation of the bishop Juan Rodríguez de Fonseca to the cathedrals of Palencia and Burgos, his last bishopric see. Four panels of this series were exhibited in Barcelona's 1929 exhibition. Between 1935-36 the chapter sold two panels to the New York Metropolitan Museum. A further panel from Palencia's

cathedral, along with another four panels of this same set which were first recorded by the Registry of Actas Capitulares (Chapter's minutes) in 1527, were all also sold between 1930 and 1932, and later purchased by the Royal Museum of Art and History in 1964. Two pieces of this set – *Justice disarmed by Mercy* [BXL1] and *Man and the Seven Deadly Sins* [BXL4] – were studied in the MODHT project.

The fantastic series known as the 'Triumphs of Petrarch' illustrates the poem *I Trionfi* written by Petrarch between 1352 and 1374. This allegoric cycle was very popular in the Low Countries from the second half of the 15th century, as shown by the series commissioned in 1454 by Giovanni de' Medici and the one purchased before 1504 by Isabella the Catholic (Isabel 'la Católica'). From the two sets added in 1507 and 1510 to the collections of Henry VIII and Cardinal Wolsey in London and Hampton Court Palace, two panels were selected for the project: *Triumph of Time*

FIGURE 2.18

Monogram of weaver Jacob Wauters in
Wine Arbours Gallery [PNM 9]. (© Patrimonio Nacional)

over Fame [HRP1]; and *Triumph of Death over Chastity* [HRP3]. They are dynamic processions of triumphal chariots over which enthroned Death and Time overturn and crush their antagonizing concepts, Chastity and Fame.[7]

Throughout the 16th century Brussels, established by the Habsburgs as the capital of the Flemish tapestry industry, supplied the descendants of Maximilian I and Mary of Burgundy with tapestries. Connected to the patronage of their daughter, Marguerite of Austria (1480-1530), are various Passion tapestries produced by Pierre van Aelst and the cartoonist Jan van Roome.[8] Four panels on the Passion of Christ – *Washing of the Feet*, *Christ before Pilate*, *Road to Calvary* and *Crucifixion* – were inherited by Charles V from his aunt Marguerite. These tapestries, described as '*fort bonne et riche tapisserie d'or et de soye*' ('extremely good and rich tapestry of gold and silk') were sent in 1526 as a wedding gift to Isabella of Portugal. The date '1507' and the signature of Van Aelst woven in the figurative area of the tapestry titled *Road to Calvary*, date this set to the second decade of the 16th century.[9] This tapestry was listed in the inventories of the Palacio Real, Madrid until the 19th century when Isabella II of Spain (1843-75) presented the first two panels of the series to the diplomat Charles A. Blanc. This was in recognition of Blanc's unconditional support when Isabella was accused of fraudulently selling jewellery belonging to the Spanish Crown.

The two tapestries *Washing of the Feet* and *Christ before Pilate* decorated the palace of the Baron Blanc in the Piazza del Popolo of Rome. After his death he bequeathed them to his two daughters, and eventually they were purchased, first by the Rijksmuseum, Amsterdam in 1959, and second by the Royal Museum of Art and History, Brussels in 1963. This left the Spanish Royal Collection with only the *Road to Calvary* and the *Crucifixion* from this 'Passion of Christ' series. Thus the inclusion in the MODHT project of *Christ before Pilate* [BXL2] from the Royal Museum of Art and History's collection was an astute decision by curator Ingrid de Meûter, enabling a complete and comparative analysis of the pieces once belonging to the Spanish collection.

Mary of Austria (1505-58), the daughter of Philip the Handsome (Felipe el Hermoso) and Joanna of Castile (Juana de Castilla), was entrusted by her brother Carlos V with governing the Low Countries from 1526 (the year her husband Juan II of Hungary died) until 1555. Under her government, Flanders went through one of its greatest periods of artistic splendour, thanks to the patronage exercised not only by the Governess, but also by the region's cities, diplomats and noblemen. The rich tapestries that decorated Mary's palace in Binche faithfully reflected this particular Flemish period, with their blend of traditional manners and the influence of the Italian classical and mannerist artistic movement. The taste of the Brussels court under Mary of Austria showed in her rich collection of tapestries, one of the most famous to come from the looms of Brussels.

Also belonging to this magnificent period of tapestry-making in Brussels, known as the Renaissance of the Low Countries, were two of the most valuable pieces studied in the project: a panel from the 'Story of Tobias' of Henry VIII and the 'Fables of Ovid' of Philip II of Spain (Felipe II). Their parallels demonstrate the wish of European courts to emulate each other. With gold and silver braid threads in the weft of both series, they are textile gems which are still regarded as rich and magnificent royal treasures in the Alcázar of Madrid and at Hampton Court Palace.

Erasmus Schets, a wealthy merchant and tapestry dealer in Antwerp, took part in the transactions for the purchase of a 'Story of Tobias', a series of eight panels woven with metal threads and purchased in 1546 by Henry VIII. He was also involved in the purchase of a copy of a silk and wool tapestry of Tobias for Mary of Hungary, woven in the manufactory of Balthazar van Vlierden[10] over cartoons of the school of the painter Bernaert van Orley.

Of the eight panels that formed the Henry VIII series, the English collection has retained only the panel titled *Tobias presents Raphael to his Father* [HRP2], the others being sold and dispersed following the death of Charles I (1600-49) during the period of the Commonwealth. This remaining panel suffered another misfortune when it was damaged during the Hampton Court Palace fire of 1986.[11] Thanks to the existence of a similar tapestry in the Spanish Royal Collection – *Tobias presents Raphael to his Father* [PNM7] – the conservation department of

Hampton Court Palace was able to restore the partially charred scene.

The 'Story of Tobias' in the Spanish Royal Collection is a silk and wool copy of the cartoons previously used for Henry VIII's analogous series. It originally belonged to Mary of Austria's collection before being bequeathed to her nephew Philip II of Spain (Felipe II) following her death. This set did not survive complete either; from the 17th century the inventories of the Royal Tapestry Manufacture, Madrid stated that the eight panels had decayed despite restoration by their Flemish *retupidores*. Only three pieces have remained complete: *Tobias presents Raphael to his Father* [PNM7], incorporated into the project, as well as *Tobias and his wife bid farewell to Raguel* and *Return of Tobias and Sarah to his Parents*. The three panels show on their selvedge a mark which was thought to indicate the workshop of Franz Raes, but was recently reattributed to Balthazar van Vlierden, a weaver involved in the transactions for the Henry VIII set (considered the principle series) and also for the copy for Mary of Austria. The book of Tobias from the Old Testament, after the Latin version of Saint Jerome, was thought by the Trent Council to be inspirational, and was incorporated into sermons and pious addresses for both catholic and protestants as a beautiful story about the ways of the divine providence and as a biblical exemplary theme for monarchic matrimony. This doctrinal perspective made the Tobias tapestries well suited for decorating nuptial chambers and royal wedding ceremonies.

If one tapestry-maker embodies the quality of Brussels' tapestries at the peak of its magnificence, it is Willem de Pannemaker (active 1535-81). The son of Pieter de Pannemaker, a weaver in the court of Marguerite of Austria, he succeeded his father as the master in charge of the workshop where the greatest tapestries of the period were woven. His mastery and ability is demonstrated by the five piece set woven in gold and silver known as the 'Fables of Ovid' series, taken from the poem *The Metamorphoses of Ovid*.

The series was woven from cartoons recently attributed to Léonard Thiry, a Flemish painter who worked in Fontainebleau between 1536 and 1540. The set was purchased in 1556 by Philip II of Spain (Felipe II) from the Antwerp merchant Pieter van der Walle. This was during his second visit to Flanders on the occasion of the abdication of his father, the Holy Emperor Charles V (Carlos V).

The five panels echo the Renaissance love affair with Greek and Roman mythology as an inspirational source for visual pleasure. The theme was well suited to providing a beautiful repertoire of masculine and female nudes appropriate for the private apartments of the sovereigns, although since their inclusion in the Royal Collection this set was regularly exhibited in public ceremonies outside the Madrid's Alcázar. Thus it adorned the Guadalupe monastery in 1576 during the meeting between Philip II of Spain (Felipe II) and his nephew Don Sebastian of Portugal.[12] Somewhat surprising given the visual content, throughout the 17th century the 'Fables of Ovid' were part of the annual procession in the Alcázar's square during Corpus Christi celebrations. This exposed the pieces to damage by wind, water and light, so that they had to undergo successive repairs at the hands of well-known *retupidores* such as Gabriel Medel (d.1651) and Pedro Blaniac (d.1668), under the supervision of the senior tapestry-makers and directors of the Oficio

Tapisserie de Basse Lisse des Gobelins, Attelier et différentes Opérations des Ouvriers emploiés à la Basse Lisse.

FIGURE 2.19

An 18th-century workshop for low-warp tapestry-weaving, from the *Encyclopédie ou Dictionnaire Raisonné des Sciences, des Arts et des Métiers* (Paris, France: Chez Braisson, *c*.1772, ed. Denis Diderot and Jean le Rond d'Alembert). (© National Museums Scotland)

de Tapicería. During the reign of Philip V of Bourbon (Felipe V de Borbon) (1700-46) the set decorated the Buen Retiro Palace in Madrid and, thanks to this, escaped the fire that burned down the Alcázar of the House of Austria in 1734.

The five panels of the 'Fables of Ovid' – *Daedalus and Icarus* [PNM1], *Jupiter and Ganymede* [PNM2], and *Neoptolemus and Polyxena* [PNM5] (the three included in the project), *Andromeda and Perseus* and *Apollo and Marsyas* – are master works of Brussels' Renaissance endorsed by the marks of Brussels in Brabant, with the monogram of Willem de Pannemaker woven in gold on the selvedge. They were later exhibited in the first Tapestry Museum of Patrimonio Nacional, established in 1950 in the San Ildefonso Palace in Segovia.

Tapestries made in Bruges

Bruges and Antwerp were great commercial centres and home to the main markets for the sale and export of Flemish tapestries. Although as manufacturing centres they were dominated by the stronghold of weavers and cartoonists established in Brussels, it was nevertheless important that their production be included in the MODHT project. From the 15th century, Bruges manufactured several important series of tapestries. The oldest – a 14-panel set on the 'Life of Saint Anatoile of Salins' – was woven between 1502 and 1505 in the workshop of Jan de Wilde and his wife Catherine Hasselet. Only three panels have survived and are cared for in the Louvre Museum.

The edict regulating the production and commerce of tapestries came into effect in Bruges in 1547, with the city symbolised by the Gothic 'B' surmounted by a crown.

The characteristic bobbin of the high warp looms, the technique that characterised its production, was soon added to the symbols. A result of recent research has been the compilation of a complete catalogue of Bruges' production that includes three of the series incorporated into the MODHT project:[13] the 'Life of the Virgin' and the surviving fragments of the *Verdure with Coat of Arms of Brugse Vrije*, both in the collection of the Bruges Musées Communaux, and the 'Story of Diana' in the Spanish Royal Collection.

Of special interest were the fragments of the armorial tapestry known as *Verdure with Coat of Arms of Brugse Vrije* [BRU1], designed as a seat cover for the aldermen or mayors in the city chambers. It was woven by Antoon Segon after the models of Willem de Hollander and Lancelot Blondeel. This piece is a good example of the luxury and wealth that tapestry represented, demonstrating also that nobles and gentry considered these luxurious textiles as precious possessions and showed them in public events of similar importance to religious and courtly ceremonies. When used as heraldic and armorial tapestries in the royal households, they decorated furniture, tables, benches and stools, and were used as saddle cloths. Because of their continuous use, these typically suffered the most degradation, so the pieces that have survived are rare and fragmentary.

In the remaining fragments and wreaths of the *Verdure with Coat of Arms of Brugse Vrije*, foliage and animal figures are on a blue background, crowns surround the heraldic motifs on their fields, and the grotesques and trophies present are also found in other similar pieces from Bruges, in museums such as the Victoria & Albert Museum in London, and the Carolino Augusteum Museum in Salzburg.

From the 13th century, Bruges' citizens have worshipped the sculptured image of the

Virgin Mary in the Hospital of Notre-Dame de la Poterie. This devotion was consolidated after the celebration of the Trent Council. This charitable institution, which existed to help pilgrims, the vulnerable and the sick, was eventually converted into the Musée Notre-Dame de la Poterie. During the second half of the 17th century it commissioned a series of hangings on the 'Miracles of Our Lady of the Poterie' [BRU3]: three panels showing miracles carried out by the Virgin following prayers to her image. These were inspired by a set of quill drawings from the end of the 15th century. Each panel illustrated six miracle scenes, explained in Dutch verse composed in the second half of the 17th century by the Jesuit Father Philippus Franciscus Taisne. The series, woven around 1630, is a clear testimony to the liturgical value of tapestry, also appreciated by those less fortunate for its narrative and figurative value.

After the refurbishment and enlargement of the Hospital, completed in 1625, a new series of two panels about the 'Life of the Virgin' was purchased as evidence of the persistence of the city's devotion to the miraculous image of the Virgin of the Poterie. Although none of the two panels has the Bruges' mark, both include the date 1639 woven on the inferior border together with a Latin inscription explaining the story represented in the figurative area. It has not been possible to find the name of the weaver or the cartoonist, although there is no doubt that a Bruges master weaver was responsible for the distinctive garlands, vases and flowers, the landscaped cartouches and the lion masks on a dark background, together with the distinctive blue and yellow shades of wools and silks characteristic of the Bruges production. The panel titled *The Annunciation* follows the narration of Saint Luke's Gospel, but the episode on *Mary's Presentation in the Temple* [BRU2] does not follow the canonical Gospels. Instead it was typical of the Christian apocrypha tradition taken from the Proto-Gospel of James, the pseudo Matthew Gospel, or the Gospel of the Nativity of the Virgin, widely known from the Middle Ages thanks to the Golden Legend of Jacobus de Voragine. There is some basis to believe that the models for the composition have been extracted, as was often done, from a Baroque repertoire of religious illustrated cards. However, current thinking relates the compositions, which have a clear influence from Caravaggio, to the Antwerp painter Pieter van Lint, or to Jacob van Oost, the Elder of Bruges.

Finally, the tapestry *Atalanta hunts the Calydonian wild boar* [PNM8], an example of Bruges manufacture, was incorporated into the MODHT project because the manufacturer's mark on its right selvedge is that of the imperial edict of 1544 described above. This panel illustrates part of the 'Story of Diana', a mythological story narrated in the poem, the *Metamorphoses of Ovid*. Although the weaver and the cartoonist are unknown, the compositions reflect the influence of the Baroque style of painting in the way the background landscape is represented, and in the anatomies and in the voluptuousness of the female clothing. For these reasons the series has been dated around 1630, although the animal figures and four elements motifs of the borders are an iconography used in the previous century, created in Bruges for the 'Story of Noah' of Philip II of Spain (Felipe II) in 1563. This signifies the persistence of the Brussels models in other Flemish workshops, and the artistic interchanges of weavers and cartoonists between the various workshops.

Tapestries made in Antwerp

During the 16th and 17th centuries, Antwerp's workshops exported Flemish tapestries to the rest of Europe; it was also an important weaving centre, although always subordinate to the activity and fame of Brussels master weavers. Antwerp production has been represented in the MODHT project with a type of tapestry known as 'Pergolas' or 'Galleries'. There are numerous mentions of series of 'Galleries' in the royal inventories of the House of Habsburg in Spain, a sign of the fashionable status of these panels. 'Galleries' panels had a decorative purpose, but also possessed an iconography that is still poorly understood. They were intended for the decoration of architectural galleries opening onto the gardens of the Buen Retiro Palace in Madrid, built by Philip IV of Spain (r.1621-65). These hangings signified the transition and connection between the horticultural world of the exterior gardens and the courtly interior spaces, a reflection of the style of the period's Baroque plays.

Regardless of the damage suffered by these 'Galleries' due to their location and exposure to light, four series of hangings have survived in the Spanish Royal Collection with variants in the structure of their templates and the composition of their borders. However, in the selvedge of one piece, *Wine Arbours Gallery* [PNM9], is the mark of Jacob Wauters.[14] This has a clear parallel with similar pieces in the Queen's Gallery at the Palace of Holyroodhouse in Edinburgh. For all these reasons, it was included in the project.

Conclusion

Selecting the right tapestries for the MODHT was as essential to the project as evaluating the right analytical methods to study them with. Careful consideration was given by collection experts to choosing 17 from some of Europe's finest collections, the selection being based on each tapestry's historical significance, collection history, accessibility and relationship to each other. The project team was exceptionally fortunate to be granted permission to sample and research such historically significant and priceless textiles.

When the project had finished, a wealth of new information had been gathered from historical sources and scientific analysis, bestowing each tapestry with increased understanding about their background, their interconnections and manufacture, and more complete collection information. This added knowledge will benefit not only the individual tapestries studied, but their collections, and others with parallels to them.

References

1. Campbell, T. (2002): *Tapestry in the Renaissance. Art and Magnificence* (New York: The Metropolitan Museum of Art).

2. Campbell, T. (2007): *Henry VIII and the Art of Majesty. Tapestries at the Tudor Court* (New Haven and London: The Paul Mellan Centre for Studies in British Art by Yale University Press).

3. Campbell, T. (1994): 'William III and "The Triumph of Lust": the tapestries hung in the King's State Apartments in 1699', in *Apollo*, no. 390, pp. 22-31.

4. At least 28 surviving choir tapestries have been catalogued (Weigert, 2004). Articles and exhibitions give evidence of the liturgical value of these tapestries and the richness of the Arras workshops' production.

   REFERENCES:
   - *Saints de Choeurs-Tapisseries du Moyen Age*, cat. d'exp. Toulouse, Ensemble conventuel des Jacobins, 24 Avril–31 Août 2004; Aix-en-Provence, *Musée des tapisseries*, Septembre–Décembre 2004; Caen, Musée de Normandie, Janvier–Mai 2005; Milan, Editions 5 Continents, 2004.
   - *Tapisseries d'Anjou (XVe-XVIIIe siècles) au Trésor de la Cathédrale de Liège*, cat. d'exp. Liège, 26 Juin–30 Septembre 2004 (Liège: Ed. du Perron, 2004).
   - Arminjon, Catherine: 'Les saints de choeur. Tentures médiévales et Renaissance', *L'Estampille-l'Objet d'Art*, 392 (Juin 2004, pp. 60-69).
   - Maupas, Audrey Nassieu: 'La Vie de saint Jean-Baptiste d'Angers et la production de tapisseries à Paris dans la première moitié du XVIe siècle', *Revue de l'Art*, 145/3 (2004), pp. 41-53.

5. Pinchart, A. (1878-85): *Histoire de la Tapisserie dans les Flandres* (Paris), pp. 5-37 and 73-83; Deshaines, Ch. (1879): *La Tapisserie de haute lisse à Arras avant le XVe siècle d'après des documents inédits* (Paris), p. 2; cf. Müntz, E. (1882): *La Tapisserie* (París), p. 109.

6. Delmarcel, G. (ed.) (1976): *Tapisseries bruxelloises de la pré-Renaissance* (Bruxelles: Musées Royaux d'Art et d'Histoire), pp. 78-83.

7. Delmarcel, G. (1989): 'Text and Image: Some Notes on the Tituli of Flemish "Triumphs of Petrarch" Tapestries', in *Textile History* (Ancient and Medieval Textiles; Studies in Honour of Donald King), 20, pp. 321-29.

8. Herrero, C. (2004): *Tapices de Isabel la Católica. Origen de la colección real* (Madrid: Patrimonio Nacional).

9. Crick-Kuntziger, M. (1936): vol. 2, p. 4, plate 146.

10. The letter 'R' of the monogram present in the selvedge linked it to Franz Raes. However, lately it has been associated by Professor Delmarcel to the weaver Balthazar van Vlierden, involved in the transaction in 1547 together with the merchant Erasmus Schets; cf. Delmarcel, G. (1999): 'Le roi Philippe II d'Espagne et la Tapisserie. L'inventaire de Madrid de 1598', in *Gazette des Beaux-Arts*, vol. 134, pp. 153-78, specifically p. 164.

11. Band, J. (1994): 'The Hampton Court fire: the conservation of the damaged textiles', in *Apollo*, no. 390, pp. 46-49.

12. Davila, A. (1954): *Felipe II y el rey don Sebastián de Portugal* (Madrid), pp. 307-11.

13. Delmarcel, G. and E. Duverger (1987): *Bruges et la tapisserie* (Mouscron-Bruges).

14. On Wauters' monogram and his activity, see Crick-Kuntziger, M. (1935): 'Contribution à l'histoire de la tapisserie anversoise: les marques et les tentures des Wauters', in *Revue belge d'archéologie et d'histoire de l'art* (RBAHA), o Belg. Tijdschr. Oudh. Kunstg., 5, pp. 35-44; Digby, G. W. (1959): 'Tapestries by the Wauters family of Antwerp for the English market', in *Herfsttij van de Vlaamse Tapijkunst* (Brussels), pp. 227-44; Duverger, E. (1977): 'Antwerp tapestries of the seventeenth century', in *Connoisseur*, April, pp. 274-87.

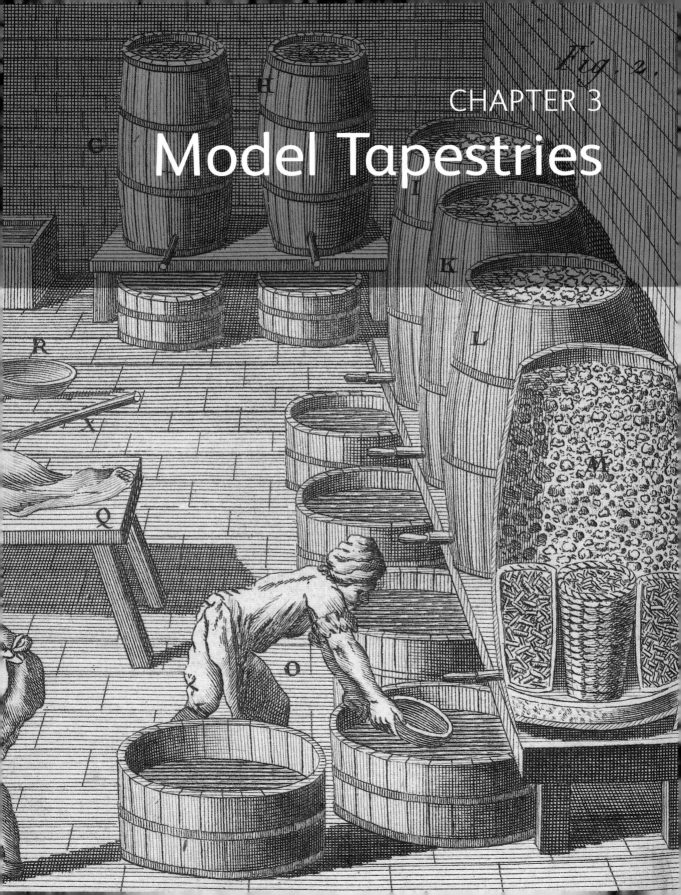

Model Tapestries

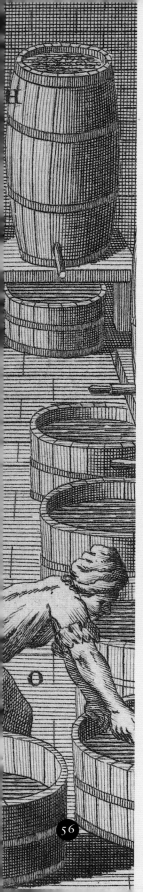

CHAPTER 3
Model Tapestries

Marei Hacke, Kathryn Hallett, David Peggie, Anita Quye and Ina Vanden Berghe

THE most noticeable effects of damage on historical tapestries are faded colours, splits in the woven structure, sagging and broken yarns. Such changes are certain to have been influenced by display environments, cleaning and preservation treatments and amount of handling, as well as the construction materials and method, but to what extent? For many years, conservators and curators have wondered how much more change can be expected, whether factors influencing present condition could still affect the tapestries, and if the extent of damage could be measured objectively rather than intuitively. Seeking answers was the essence of the MODHT project.

Fundamental to the project was finding a way to start at the beginning, so to speak, of a tapestry's life, so that the effects of dyes, yarns and metals, dyeing and weaving processes, and environmental exposure (to light, temperature and humidity) on its strength could be followed. To achieve this ambitious aim, replicas were made using traditional materials and techniques. As can be imagined, this was no easy feat and required a lot of time, knowledge and patience to be as historically accurate as possible. In some instances lateral thinking was called for, such as converting a hatful (specifically a felt one) of bran quoted in a 16th-century dyeing recipe into metric units, and modifying the threading of a modern mechanical loom – even then, over a century old – so that the weaving method used over 400 years ago was faithfully reproduced in the shortest time.

In this chapter, the making, ageing and testing of the model tapestries and metal threads, and analytical technique development, are described. The results are summarised to show the trends relating to different dye and fibre effects. These results were then compared to those observed for the historical tapestries.

History of tapestries

Weaving a tapestry was a highly complex and laborious process. The commission was initiated with painters delivering designs to *kartonniers* who increased the scale and transformed every detail to create a template (cartoon) for the weavers to follow.[1]

Two weaving techniques were traditionally used. One involved tracing the cartoon onto vertical warps, with the weaver working from the back of the tapestry and stepping in front of the loom to see progress. The other involved a loom with foot pedals, horizontal warps and the cartoon placed underneath, leaving the weaver with both hands free for inserting the weft and making the process faster. In both cases the pattern emerged from coloured weft yarns (wool and silk) interlacing over and under the warp yarns, which were almost always wool.

The quality of materials and production was paramount. English wool was best, while silk was mainly Italian and Spanish. Metallic threads often originated from Italy or Cyprus.[2] Dyeing could be done in the importing country, but only by master dyers. Originally the colour palette was limited to a few shades of red, blue, yellow and green. Renaissance tapestries from Brussels were the first to show pink, mauve and very light blue. By the sixteenth century, French and Flemish weavers had perfected a technique called *hachures*, blending colours by interlinking different coloured yarns and thereby extending the colour range [see Figure 3.2]. Flemish Renaissance tapestries were often rich in gold and silver threads, a trademark for certain makers such as Bernaert van Orley.[3] As imagined, quality tapestries were only affordable by the very rich.

Guilds for tapestry-makers put in place strict quality controls, such as ensuring that

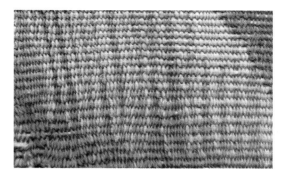

FIGURE 3.1 (pages 54 to 55, and opposite)

Dyeing textiles black in an 18th-century workshop, from the *Encyclopédie ou Dictionnaire Raisonné des Sciences, des Arts et des Métiers* (Paris, France: Chez Braisson, c.1772, ed. Denis Diderot and Jean le Rond d'Alembert). (© National Museums Scotland)

FIGURE 3.2 (above)

Detail of tapestry weave showing *hachures* technique. (© Historic Royal Palaces)

weavers initialled their work in the border, and forbidding iron-containing dyes for black because the yarn decayed quickly. Dark brown and dark blue were supposed to be substitutes, but the missing black outlines of images even in the best surviving tapestries suggest this was not always followed. Painting or embroidering details, like faces, was regarded as cheating, and so was not permitted either. The powerful guilds also administered penalties. In one instance in 1539 a large quantity of reputedly inferior tapestries belonging to Willem de Kempeneer, a prominent master weaver in Brussels, was confiscated and a fine added for good measure.

The sheer size of large-scale tapestries put considerable tension onto the warps during weaving. The resulting shrinkage when the tapestry was finally cut off the loom affected the visual appearance of the design, especially of figures. By weaving in the horizontal direction rather than vertical, as normal for other woven textiles, distortion was less noticeable, but meant that the tapestry's wefts bore most of the weight when hanging.

FIGURE 3.3

Examples of the brightly-coloured naturally-dyed
model tapestry specially made for the research project.
(© Historic Royal Palaces)

Wefts did not run the whole width of the fabric because they had to be changed for each different colour. The resulting slits were sewn with loose ends of yarn by the weaver when finished. Although incredibly strong when new, centuries of ageing and supporting its weight make a tapestry vulnerable to splitting, especially in the weft direction.

Making the model tapestries

Wool and silk yarns

The purpose of making tapestries with materials and methods true to the originals was to create models for controlled testing. Textile conservators at Hampton Court Palace reviewed a wide selection of available modern yarns before purchasing the English sheep wool for the warps, and Italian-sourced spun cultivated silk (*Bombyx Mori*) for the wefts.[4] Before use, the wool had been degreased and the silk degummed using traditional methods.[5]

Dyes and dyeing

When the historical tapestries investigated in the project were made, dyes would have come from natural sources like plants and insects. A natural dye is essentially a mixture of coloured chemicals that provide a chemical profile for the source, such as the species of plant it came from. This signature, relating to the number, relative amounts and certain properties of the chemicals in the mixture, is remarkably consistent, to the point that a dye in a textile made over 500 years ago can be identified from plants growing today.

DYES FOR THE MODELS

Natural dyes are normally extracted from their source by soaking in water, except indigo and woad which need special processing. Chemicals named in brackets are the typical mordant for the dye (alum is the common name for aluminium potassium sulfate).

Model tapestries treated with mordants only were also prepared, to investigate any significant effects they had on the textiles.

Madder *Rubia tinctoria*

- Roots of a plant native to Europe and Asia.
- Colours: red and orange (alum), purple and brown (iron sulfate).

Cochineal *Dactylopius coccus*

- A scale insect native to South America, brought to Europe in the early 16th century and cultivated. Prized for its excellent bright colour and high dye content.
- Colours: red (alum); pink and bright red (tin chloride, from 17th century onwards).

Brazilwood *Caesalpinia species*

- Heartwood of two species of tree: *C. sappan* (Asia) and *C. brasilensis* (South America). It faded easily, so use was legally controlled to ensure colour quality.
- Colours: Pink and brown (alum).

Weld *Reseda luteola*
and dyer's greenweed *Genista tinctoria*

- Stems and leaves of native European plants, giving a bright yellow.

- Dyer's greenweed is more prone to fading than weld.
- Colours: yellow (alum); green (iron sulfate or copper sulfate).

Sawwort *Serratula spp.*

- Stems and leaves of a native European plant, giving a bright yellow. Historically documented alongside dyer's greenweed as a common substitute for weld.[6]
- Colours: yellow (alum); green (iron sulfate or copper sulfate).

Young fustic *Cotinus coggygria*

- Heartwood of a native European tree. Colour fades easily, but was used to colour the silk core yarn for metal threads.
- Colour: yellow (alum).

Woad *Isatis tinctoria*
and indigoid *Indigofera tinctoria*

- Both are leaves of plants. Although native to different parts of the world (woad to Europe, indigo to Asia), their dyes have the same chemical composition, so cannot be differentiated by current routine analytical methods.
- Colour: blue (no mordant needed).

Galls

- Growths on trees, especially oak, made by parasitic wasps. The dye contains natural iron components, so does not require a mordant.
- Colour: brown-black (no additional mordant needed).

BOX 1

Before the project began, dye analysis of a significant number of European tapestries indicated that nine sources were consistently used [see BOX 1]. From this seemingly limited number of dyes, dyers created an amazingly wide palette of colours by selecting different mordants (inorganic salts to bond the dye to the fibre), over-dyeing one colour with another (green from yellow and blue), adding chemicals in the dyeing process, and dyeing until no dye remained in the liquor. This enriched the tapestries with incredible colour complexity which, combined with the quality of painters and *kartonniers* used for the design, make them the textile artwork equivalents to fine paintings. The nine common dyes were selected for the model tapestries, along with the mineral iron sulfate, commonly used for black although known by the makers to damage the fibres relatively quickly. Some materials proved hard to source, but fortunately colleagues at Kew Gardens in England, and the Association Garance in France's Provence, could provide alder tree and young fustic respectively. The correct biological source for all dyestuffs was verified by scientific analysis by KIK and NMS.

Mordanting and dyeing recipes were based on medieval practices,[7] followed as closely as health and safety regulations permitted. Parameters like weight, volume of water, pH, temperature and time were controlled and recorded for reference. Listed in appendix 2 at the end of this publication are the dye-stuffs, additives, suppliers, mordanting and dyeing recipes.

Weaving

To ensure weave uniformity in the model tapestries for scientific testing, there was little option but to use a mechanised 1905 Northrop shuttle loom at the UoM. Warp and weft yarns needed to be reversed to achieve the traditional high weft density. This made the process difficult and slow, but it was satisfying that the conservators at HRP verified the historical weave had been replicated as closely as possible [see Fig. 3.4].

The end result was 24 single colour lengths of woven wool tapestry fabric and 18 of silk, each measuring approximately 6 m long and 15 cm wide. A portion of each was distributed to each partner, the majority being sent to KIK who became the primary custodian for the models when the project ended (and since then also used in another European-funded project – EU-ARTECH). As well as reference materials, a better insight into how the originals were made and respectful appreciation for the skill involved was gained.

FIGURE 3.4

The weave structure of the model tapestry (above) replicated historic examples closely (below).
(© Historic Royal Palaces)

Model metal threads

Threads of silver and gold are found in the best quality tapestries. They were made by coiling strips of metal foils around a supporting core of silk yarn dyed yellow with (invariably) young fustic and/or brazilwood. The fineness and intricate structure of individual threads is intriguing. Surprisingly little is known about their manufacture and trade despite the dedication of many publications in conservation science to the study of their corrosion.[8-23] Tarnished metals blemish a tapestry's appearance, so elucidating causes and effects would help to understand and control further deterioration.

Model metal threads were made in collaboration with Goldenthreads, a unique surviving UK maker. For the core yarn, silk was dyed with young fustic and six strands of silk were twisted together. A wire of 85μm diameter (electroplated copper, silver [1%] and gold [0.5% or 2%]), was flattened between steel rollers, and the ribbon-like metal thread was mechanically wrapped around the core. The threads were then studied by the KIK.

Accelerated light ageing

The quantities of model tapestries and metal threads produced were much greater than the small samples permitted from museum textiles. This enabled refinement of the analytical techniques before application to the historical tapestries, but first the models had to undergo similar ageing effects as their older counterparts. This was made possible by exposing selected model tapestries and metal threads to controlled conditions that accelerated the effect, using light, a constant temperature and relative humidity (air moisture). Thus changes in colour, corrosion

and strength of single yarns and bulk structure could be measured and monitored. By comparing aged and unaged examples, the rate of change was also measurable, allowing predictions for the ageing of historical textiles.

The historical tapestries in this project were designed for display, so the greatest single factor weakening the materials has been exposure to light. The type and amount of damage has also depended on the wavelength of light, temperature and relative humidity, whether the yarn is wool or silk, and how it has been processed and manufactured.

The project required two different levels of accelerated light ageing for the model samples: one to reproduce damaging conditions for the dyestuffs; and the other under harsher conditions to decay the fibres. The type of light and its intensity level determined the level of degradation. Both regimes followed methods already tested for museum-displayed historical dyed textiles (a full discussion of accelerated ageing methods can be found elsewhere).[24]

For the dye-related investigations, individual yarn samples were threaded across acid-free card and placed for specific periods of time in a purpose-made cabinet of inert materials, fitted with twelve fluorescent light bulbs to simulate daylight through glass and a fan to regulate the temperature.

For the fibres, woven fabric strips in holders were aged in a commercially-available industrial apparatus with xenon arc lamps to mimic daylight through window glass. It took a higher dose of light exposure to simulate decay in the yarns compared to the dyestuffs. The characteristics of light degradation were then explored by comparing the analytical results for unaged and accelerated-aged samples. Since all the different model samples received an identical exposure when aged in this way, the factors responsible for making the dyes and fibres more vulnerable to degradation could be compared.

The research aimed to separate out and investigate the effects of light on fibres and dyes, at both macro- and molecular-level, using analytical techniques to investigate how the components in new materials changed with ageing. The project team were confident that the scientific techniques would be able to identify micro-level damage in very small samples, before any measurable physical evidence of weakening on the macro-level.

Understanding the materials

Fibres

The fundamental building blocks of wool and silk are amino acids, bonded together to form proteins, which are themselves linked chemically to form long chains called polymers. Collectively these polymers form the fibres. The main protein in wool is keratin, and that for silk is fibroin. With ageing the protein composition can change, causing the chains to break chemically into shorter lengths and thus individual fibres to lose strength. *En masse* this causes the textile to tear or fall apart. The effect of sunlight on wool is that over-exposure causes shedding of fibres as the keratin breaks down. With silk, the result is fibroin breaking into smaller and smaller pieces, known as 'shattering'.

Fibre weakness is unfortunately one of the most damaging effects on tapestries, so identifying areas with low strength or monitoring changes before visible damage occurs to the tapestry was a key aim for the project. Ultimately areas can become so weakened

that handling the textile causes rips and tears to appear. This is one of the dangers for historical tapestries. If change is consistent and detectable, the vulnerable amino acids become useful damage markers.

Dyes

Dyes exposed to too much light may ultimately change colour, eventually fading as the chemical bonds of their molecules alter or breakdown. Damage by light (photodegradation) is visually most striking in old tapestries where leaves and grass have turned blue, a consequence of preferential fading by the yellow dyes originally present in combination with the blue dye to create green.

Although yellow plant dyes generally tend to fade quickly, they vary between themselves depending on the type of chemicals, called flavonoids, present in them. For example, weld is relatively more stable than dyer's greenweed, and both are more stable than another dye called quercitron bark.[25] Red dyes with the related chemicals called neoflavonoids (in brazilwood and other redwood dyes[26]) are likewise much more likely to fade than the red dyes cochineal and madder, which contain the more fade-resistant chemicals called anthraquinones. Brazilwood was sometimes used for flesh tones in tapestries, so fading can lead to odd effects in tapestries, like outstanding bright red lips on almost invisible faces.

Because a dye's characteristic components and their relative amounts identify its biological species, significant differences between the results from aged and unaged yarns can prevent identification. It is sometimes possible to piece together information from the altered chemicals to work back to the original composition, as extensive analytical research to identify the profile of photo-degraded quercitron bark and other flavonoid dyes has shown.[27] It was therefore important to investigate how the analytical results would differ for the yellow dyes in the historical tapestries – weld, dyer's greenweed and possibly sawwort [see BOX 1, page 59] – and to evaluate the usefulness of the resulting analytical profiles for providing information about levels of damage.

Being able to identify the source of a natural dye can also provide historical information for where or when a historical yarn was dyed,[28] and similar results could prove useful for grouping tapestries by how or where they were made.

Analytical methods

Model tapestry materials and metal threads were used to perfect analytical methods or understand more about the chemistry of the materials. It was especially important to ensure that scientific tests were not only possible but valid for the small samples normally available from only the reverse side of a tapestry.

Analytical tests to measure tensile strength and to identify amino acid composition for fibres were already well-established before the project started, so the models enabled these methods to be applied to identifying markers of damage, then honed to minimise sample size. Other techniques were improved or applied for the first time, such as measuring the average chain length of silk and non-destructive screening of fibres to identify surface chemical changes as damage markers. Analysis of the models also enabled the first systematic and controlled study of the effect of dyeing on the strength of fibres, to see whether dyeing conditions would have weakened the historical tapestries even when new.

Fibres

Physical properties

The lengths of keratin and fibroin polymers significantly influence how much they can be stretched or pulled before breaking. By analysing and comparing different model tapestries' yarns before and after accelerated ageing, fibre strengths could be tested in different ways and trends compared to the results from historical samples for interpretation of meaningful and measurable damage.

Establishing the physical properties of a tapestry, such as tensile strength (the behaviour of a material under an applied load) is an important part of condition assessment. However, reliable measurements require large sample sizes to be destroyed and many repeat measurements. Tensile strength tests could therefore be applied only to model tapestry samples, not historical ones. This meant that micro-analytical techniques to identify chemical markers of damage relating to physical strength had to be developed (described on page 68).

The tensile strength of the model samples was measured according to a British Standard for such tests.[29] The test measures the maximum force to which the textile can be subjected before it starts to fail, and also the increase in length after application of force. Most tapestries are designed to hang with the warp direction horizontal and the weft direction vertical. The samples for tensile strength testing were therefore prepared so that they would be tested in the same way, to simulate the forces experienced by a hung tapestry.

FIGURE 3.5

Mounting a model tapestry sample for tensile strength testing. (© Historic Royal Palaces)

Chemical properties

Keratin and fibroin are formed from chemical units called amino acids. Their different composition imparts different properties, and subtle variations between wool and silk source can be differentiated by chemical analysis [BOX 2, opposite]. For the project, analytical methods were used that produced chemical profiles as a signature for the damage in the fibre's amino acids. Importantly, these methods could be performed on a much smaller sample than needed for traditional tensile strength tests, and so were appropriate for the historical tapestries.

Importantly for the tapestry project, physical damage of the fibres caused by prolonged exposure to oxygen and light could be linked to changes in certain specifically sensitive amino acids. From previous research, the amino acids cystine and cysteic acid looked as if they would be useful as damage indicators for wool, so the analysis centred on improving ways to measure them. But, for silk there was no similar marker previously identified, so the analysts had to discover how best to measure meaningful change in silk as well as wool.

Metal threads

Metal thread corrosion was investigated by a standard museum method called the 'Oddy test'.[30] This is an accelerated corrosion test which involves placing a material sample into a test tube with small pieces of metal foil (typically one piece each of silver, copper and lead, referred to as coupons). A small amount of purified water is also placed inside the test tube, and the sealed tube is put into an oven at 60°C. The contents of the tube are examined after one month to see if the metal coupons have been tarnished by gases emitted by the test material. High temperature and humidity increase the rate at which chemical reactions occur, so the Oddy test helps to predict the type of corrosion which might happen between a metal and material over a much longer time in normal conditions.

For this research the test was adapted slightly to study the effect of tapestry silk and wool yarns on metal threads. Silver and copper coupons were incubated with some of the dyed wool and silk samples, to study how heat and light damage to the fibres could induce corrosion, and to compare with what we could observe on historic metal threads.

FIGURE 3.6 (opposite page)

Part of a HLPC system, used for separating mixtures. (© Historic Royal Palaces)

SEPARATING MIXTURES

Chromatography separates chemical mixtures and is an extremely useful analytical tool for fibre proteins and dyes. Connection to a spectroscopic or spectrometric detector allows measurement of specific properties for each separated chemical, such as light-absorbing characteristics, mass or polymer length. Sample sizes are acceptably small for museum applications, varying from an eye-lash length yarn for dye analysis to a printed full-stop sized sample for amino acid analysis. Curators and conservators are always pleased when technique development reduces sample sizes even further, so long as the results are still meaningful.

Most applications require the sample in solution, so pre-treatment with different solvents is necessary to either extract the dye out of the fibre, or dissolve a fibre's proteins or break them down further into amino acids. Amino acids also need to be tagged with a fluorescing chemical before analysis to make detection easier.[31]

For the tapestry project, dyes and amino acids were best analysed by liquid chromatography, technically speaking high pressure or high performance (abbreviated to HPLC). In each case, the chromatographic system comprises of a solvent flowing through a column containing a material appropriate to the sample type. For dyes and amino acids, the column material is chemically-modified silica with the mixture components separating by their differing affinities for the solvent or the column material. For polymer length measurement, size exclusion chromatography (SEC) was used, with the material in the column being porous beads that trap polymers for different times depending on their length.

Shorter length polymers can move in and out of the porous beads, taking more time to pass through the column than longer polymers.[32] In all cases, components are differentiated by the time each is retained before detection (retention time).

Dyes are coloured because their components absorb visible light, so the spectroscopic detector (a photodiode array (PDA)) measures light-absorbing properties for each chromatographed component. It is also useful to measure the mass of the separated dye components using a technique called liquid chromatography-mass spectrometry (LC-MS). For amino acids the detector measures their fluorescing properties, and for the polymers, their ultraviolet light absorption properties. Under controlled conditions, the combination of retention time and spectroscopic measurement is consistent for each component and often unique, although each identification relies on matching the result with that of known reference materials.

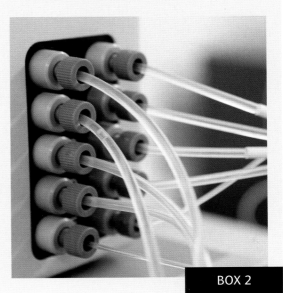

BOX 2

SURFACE ANALYSIS

When a tapestry or any other type of object suffers photodegradation, the chemical reactions start at the surface – closest to the light. Some scientific methods allow the examination of only the outer surface of a sample. Such techniques are very sensitive and good for measuring 'early-stage' damage, because they can detect chemical change at the surface even if the damage has not yet reached the bulk of the material. Accordingly, fibre damage can be investigated by identifying and measuring changes in chemical bonds on a fibre's surface. Infrared (IR) spectroscopy is a common technique for this, whereby infrared light is directed onto the sample and the characteristic vibration of the surface molecules measured.[33] Because infrared light cannot shine all the way through tapestry fibres, a diamond crystal was used to direct the infrared beam to the sample surface, and then reflect it back to the equipment's detector. This variation on regular IR spectroscopy is called 'attenuated total reflection' (ATR).[34] It had already been used to study the oxidation products of cystine in wool (such as cysteic acid).[35]

As well as chemical bonds, the relative amounts of elements at the surface of a fibre can change after photodegradation. One way to study this is by scanning electron microscopy (SEM), which provides very high magnification images of a sample by scanning an electron beam across a surface and collecting the signal from the interaction of the beam and sample surface.[36] As the electron beam strikes the sample, X-rays with characteristic energy are emitted; these can be used to identify which chemical elements are present on the sample surface in a technique called 'energy dispersive X-ray microanalysis' (EDX).

Two further specialised techniques are even more surface sensitive, and involve bombarding the sample with different types of beam and measuring the distinctive substances emitted. X-ray photoelectron spectroscopy (XPS) uses a beam of X-ray photons, which cause electrons to be released from the sample.[37] The energy of these electrons is measured, and is characteristic of each element and its chemical state. Comparison of carbon, oxygen and sulfur ratios offered potentially useful markers of surface oxidation. Secondary ion mass spectrometry (SIMS) uses a beam of (typically) gallium ions, which causes the sample to emit atoms, molecules and molecular fragments. Below a threshold beam level, the sample surface remains intact and the method is 'static', but if the beam is repeatedly scanned across an area the surface erodes and the method is 'dynamic'. Elemental variation can be monitored as a function of depth into the sample.[38] These techniques all require very small samples (the size of a printed full stop), and often the sample can be recovered for use in other tests afterwards.

BOX 3

FIGURE 3.7 (opposite page)

Model tapestry samples (unaged, left, and artificially aged, right) after tensile strength testing. (© Historic Royal Palaces)

Dyes and colour

Dyes were analysed by an analytical method very similar to that for amino acid analysis, providing chemical profiles relating to their source [see BOX 2]. Although analysis helped ensure the right biological sources for the natural dyes, the principal use was to investigate the chemical changes to dyes after the model tapestries had been aged.

The colour of the model tapestries was accurately measured before and after accelerated ageing using a spectrophotometer. This equipment provides a set of three co-ordinates for any colour, which precisely describes the location of that colour in a three-dimensional colour 'sphere'. The difference in these colour co-ordinates after exposure of a sample to light can then be calculated, giving a scientific measure of how much the colour has changed.[39] This is more accurate than comparing against colour charts (Pantones) for example.

Investigating the models

Tensile strength testing

Tensile strength testing gave broad, but nonetheless very useful, information about the different physical properties of silk and wool. Before ageing, the silk model tapestries were much stronger than the wool model tapestries. But with accelerated light ageing, the silk degraded much more rapidly than the wool, so that the silk model tapestries ended up weaker. On the other hand, wool model tapestries were stretchier and less stiff than silk: the application of an identical load would cause greater stretching in wool than silk. This was as expected, given the difference in micro-structure of wool (helical, like a coiled spring) and silk (pleated sheets). This difference is important because silk often forms the most vulnerable part of a tapestry: weft fibres which are load-bearing in a hanging tapestry as well as forming the image.

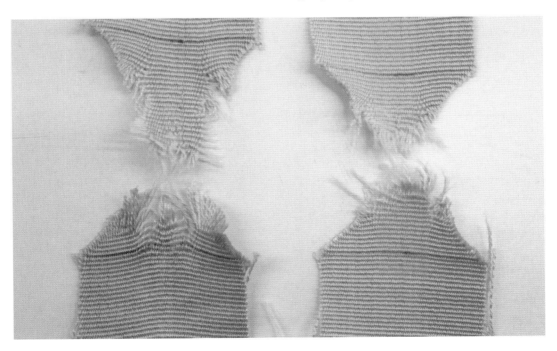

Trends in tensile strength for the woven model tapestries matched those of single yarns dyed and aged in the same way. For unaged samples, any difference in strength between the samples is down to processing techniques. This may be the dye or mordant used, or whether the dyeing conditions such as pH or temperature were more aggressive. All the model tapestries showed a big decrease in strength after accelerated light ageing. Even though tensile strength tests generally indicate significant structural changes, there was still a relative scale of strength after accelerated ageing.

The results of the tensile strength tests showed that most of the differently dyed wool and silk model samples had fairly similar physical properties. However, the unaged samples which stretched the least before breaking were the samples treated with black dye. This indicated that a factor associated with the black dye formulation (iron salt and oak gall) or dyeing conditions caused inherent damage to the fibres, compared with undyed fibres. The red silk tapestry dyed with cochineal, copper turnings and oak gall – the latter two of which may have increased fibre vulnerability – was also weaker.

In contrast, the woad-dyed samples (both for wool and silk) were strongest. The woad dye process may be considered the least aggressive in terms of lower temperature and higher (more alkaline) pH. In fact, woad-dyed silk even appeared to degrade at a slower rate than undyed silk, suggesting that the unusual ring-dye mechanism of woad may have some protective effect against light for the dyed fibres.

Tensile tests also suggested that mordants had an influence on yarns. The oak gall mordant was most detrimental to physical strength, and the alum mordant was the most benign, alder bark mordant having an intermediate effect. Oak gall mordant also has a particularly damaging effect on wool during light ageing. It is suggested that in oak galls, iron in its ferric form (Fe^{3+}) is a photosensitiser, indirectly increasing the light energy absorbed by the fibres. The addition of lye (potassium carbonate) did not seem to have an effect on strength.

Mechanical testing was also performed using smaller samples and loads by dynamic mechanical analysis (DMA). Several modes of operation could be used, providing complementary information to the tensile tester, a measure of the extension of model wool and silk tapestry samples when subjected to a linear increase in relative humidity (up to 80 per cent), and a measure of the temperature dependence of the viscoelastic properties of model wool and silk and some historical wool samples.[40]

Chemical analysis of the fibres

There was a linear relationship between average polymer chain length (measured using size exclusion chromatography [SEC]) and the elongation (stretchiness) of fibres. As expected, the average polymer length of all silk model tapestries was significantly lower following accelerated ageing because exposure to light had caused polymer chains to break. The model silk tapestries which exhibited the shortest average chain length were those dyed: black; with oak galls; and with cochineal. The least change was measured for woad-dyed silk.

Quantification of oxidised and non-oxidised sulfur by X-ray photoelectron spectroscopy (XPS) was also found to be a useful marker in wool with good correlation to tensile strength. This is a useful way to measure the strong disulfide bonds in wool (cystine: disolfide bond between two cysteine amino acids), which break after oxidation.[41]

Analysis of the amino acid composition of the wool model samples showed that oxidation, a key damage mechanism, can be measured as a decrease of the basic amino acids and an increase of the acidic ones.[42] A decrease of the amino acid tyrosine and an increase of cysteic acid were particularly useful markers. A high increase in cysteic acid was noticed for the unaged and aged black wool dyed with a mixture of iron and copper sulfates. This indicates that these two metal salts particularly affect the chemical degradation of proteins.

Changes in the amino acid composition of the silk model samples were more difficult to measure; for silk, the ratio of basic to acidic amino acids is not relevant as the specific amino acids are only present in very small quantities in fibroin (the protein in silk). So, for silk samples, a decrease in tyrosine was the only reliable marker for oxidative degradation. In general, dyeing conditions caused less degradation to the silk models than the wool ones. In contrast, degradation caused by accelerated ageing was generally higher for the silk.

ATR-FTIR analysis provided evidence that mordanting, in particular with oak gall, causes a more pronounced cysteic acid signal (indicative of more oxidation-related damage). Similarly to the amino acid analysis results, the series of the black dyed wool samples dyed using iron and copper salts, and oak gall, also had higher cysteic acid values, but the black samples mordanted with alder bark were not as damaged. Secondary ion mass spectroscopy (SIMS) confirmed the relative increase in cysteic acid on the wool surface following accelerated ageing, which was also shown to reduce the relative amount of surface fatty acids/lipids.

Comparative data between the different scientific techniques showed good agreement between the results of SEC, amino acid analysis, and ATR-FTIR and XPS surface analysis. The techniques revealed complementary information which could be combined to evaluate theories based on observational evidence. For example, black dyes are of particular interest to conservators because they are often missing or extremely weak. This was underpinned by the results, with black model samples showing significant change in all marker values even before any light exposure. This means the dyeing alone was sufficiently aggressive to cause measurable degradation. Black fibres are inherently weak from manufacture, and light exposure worsens the decay process compared to other dyestuffs. Data for woad-dyed samples also corroborated the observation that blue woad-dyed areas of historic tapestries are long-lasting.

Metal corrosion

Under the conditions applied in the Oddy tests, degradation by light caused greater metal thread tarnishing than thermal degradation, with the degradation of wool being more corrosive than the degradation of silk. There were no apparent differences in levels of corrosion due to the different dyes in the thermal tests. The more extensive tarnishing with the darker shades of wool in the light exposure tests were tentatively attributed to greater light absorption, resulting in higher loss of gaseous sulfur species due to damage to the keratin.

Colour measurement

A link between the colour change (fading) of the model tapestries measured before and after accelerated ageing and tensile strength was found. This relationship was measured on strictly controlled model samples, but because there were so many dye recipe variations, colour change alone could not be a reliable indicator of strength loss in a historic tapestry. The colour measurement results confirmed previously published research on how vulnerable the different dyestuffs were to light-fading. The greatest amount of fading was measured for the brazilwood-dyed wool samples, and least for those dyed black or with woad. The presence of lye in any dye recipe did not seem to make a difference to the colour change. The comparison between fading of the same dyestuff on silk and wool was also studied, revealing that weld applied to silk faded less on wool.

Dye analysis

The effect of the dyeing process on the chemical composition of a dye was most evident for dyer's greenweed. The ratio of its flavonoids (genistein, luteolin and apigenin) was found to be highly dependent on the dyeing process, most noticeably for genistein which decreased with respect to the other components as the number of repeat dyeings increased. Natural variation of the relative flavonoid abundances found in the dye plant material may also affect the relative ratios of colouring components observed in the extracts of dyed yarns, although different batches of dyestuff were not examined in this study.

After accelerated ageing, all dyes except sawwort and brazilwood were identifiable from their original chemical profile. With sawwort, its chemical profile after photodegradation resembled weld's. From the perspective of a tapestry exposed to light for 400 or 500 years, this would make it difficult to distinguish confidently between them. Hence sawwort, a documented common dye, would easily be overlooked by chemical analysis.

Brazilwood photodegrades to leave a chemical marker which, although studied thoroughly by UoE and NMS, unfortunately eluded full chemical characterisation during this project.[43] The study, however, proved it was a consistently reliable indicator for brazilwood and therefore would be looked for in the historical samples.

Based on past analyses, young fustic was expected to be the only yellow dye for the yarn (normally silk), around which metal threads were wrapped (see section on 'Model metal threads' above). Being so photo sensitive, it was very unlikely to have been used for wool and silk yarns exposed to light. Its photodegradation was therefore of less importance than its chemical characterisation. The main components were already known (sulfuretin and fisetin), but the project offered the opportunity to attempt the identification of the minor characterising components. Unfortunately the levels were so low that it could only be speculated that these related to dihydrofisetin, another minor component of young fustic, so further investigative work is required.

The chemical composition of sawwort and cochineal were also intensively examined in this project to more fully identify their characterising composition. A component in cochineal, referred to as dcII since identification in 1987 but with chemical structure unknown,[44] was found to be structurally related to carminic acid by mass spectrometry with a similar UV-Visible spectrum to flavokermesic acid. Two other unknowns – dcIV and dcVII – were found to be isomers of carminic acid, most probably differing only in the stereochemistry of the sugar attached to the molecule.[45]

Conclusion

From the accelerated ageing trials, we confirmed that it takes a lot more (light) energy to cause damage to the fibres when compared to the dyes, which fade more easily. However, even if dyes have not faded much, the fibres may still have been damaged by other causes. For instance, wool degradation was initiated during the mordanting and dyeing process, and depended on both the dyestuffs/mordants and the process conditions (pH, temperature). The dyes and additives in the dye bath itself seemed to be the main cause of fibre damage during the dye process of the yarns, more than the mordant used or the high temperature of the dyeing. It appeared that silk fibres are less influenced by the dyeing and mordanting, but more by the light ageing. Being able to identify the dye is important for predicting areas in a tapestry which may be predisposed to damage, but the different damage mechanisms for dyes and fibres should be considered separately.

The key differences between wool and silk degradation are that silk starts off stronger than wool, but ages more rapidly and ends up weaker. The swift nature of silk degradation may be particularly catastrophic for tapestries because silk is usually present in the weft direction, which carries both the pictorial design and the weight of the hanging textile.

The results backed up and explained anecdotally and historically reported phenomena about the effect of dyestuffs on fibres. By discussing findings with conservators and curators, the experimental findings were compared to common observations. For example, black-dyed samples were consistently of a low strength. This fits with the common observation by conservators that the black and dark brown yarns often used to weave outlines for figures tend to be extremely weak or even missing.

The tensile strength data was compared with results from the chemical analysis to see how chemical changes which occur as a tapestry degrades might weaken the physical strength. An important aim of the research was to find chemical 'markers of damage' which would match with the results of physical testing. The tensile strength tests provided the evidence for more serious deterioration, so it was hoped that the chemical markers would be more sensitive thereby detecting damage at an earlier stage.

The range of scientific methods we used to study fibre degradation essentially provided us with different routes to the same answer. This helpfully corroborated the conclusions, but also showed that one or two techniques are sufficient for providing the information of interest to this project. From the models, trends in changes to the materials and the effect of light on them enabled predictions to be made about the historical samples. From the various analytical techniques tried on sample sizes appropriate for historical tapestries, amino acid analysis, SEC, ATR-FTIR and PDA-HPLC were chosen as the most useful for identifying damage in fibres and dyes. The real proof would be applying these predictions to the historical samples.

References

1. Ysselsteyn, D. G. T.v. (1969): *Tapestry* (The Hague, Brussels: Van Goor Zonen); Campbell, T. P. (2002): *Tapestry in the Renaissance, Art and Magnificence* (New York: The Metropolitan Museum of Art).

2. Campbell (2002): ibid.

3. Hunter, G. L. (1925): *The Practical Book of Tapestries* (Philadelphia & London: J. B. Lippincott Company).

4. Rapp-Buri and Stucky-Schuerer (2001): *Burgundische Tapisserien* (Hirmer Verlag GmbH), p. 420; Bilson, T., Cooke, B. and D. Howell (1997): 'Mechanical Aspects of Lining "Loose Hung" Textiles', in *Fabric of an Exhibition, NAATC (North American Area Textile Conservation)* (Ottawa), pp. 1-14.

5. Hacke, A-M. (2006): 'Investigation into the Nature and Ageing of Tapestry Materials', *PhD Thesis* (University of Manchester).

6. Cardon, D. (2006): *Natural Dyes*, 2nd edition (London: Archetype).

7. De Nie, W. L. J. (1937): *De Ontwikkeling der Noord-Nederlandsche Textielververij van de Veertiende tot de Achttiende Eeuw*, transcripts from: Tbouck van Wondre (Brussel, 1513) and manuscripts from early 17th century with dyeing recipes of the Six and Kerspin Family (Holland) (Leiden); Edelstein, S. M. (1969): *The Plictho of Gioanventura Rosetti* (Cambridge: M.I.T. Press), trans. 1548 (1st) edition.

8. Braun-Ronsdorf, M. (1961): 'Gold and Silver Fabrics from Medieval to Modern Times', in *C.I.B.A. Review*, vol. 3, pp. 2-16.

9. Hoke, E. and I. Petrascheck-Heim (1977): 'Microprobe Analysis of Gilded Silver Threads from Mediaeval Textiles', *Studies in Conservation*, vol. 22, pp. 49-62.

10. Indictor, N. and C. Blair (1990): 'The Examination of Metal from Historic Indian Textiles Using Scanning Electron Microscope-Energy Dispersive X-Ray Spectrometry', in *Textile History*, 21(2), pp. 149-63.

11. Járó, M. (1990): 'Gold Embroidery and Fabrics in Europe: XI-XIV Centuries', in *Gold Bulletin*, 23(2), pp. 40-57.

12. Montegut, D., *et al.* (1992): 'Examination of Metal Threads From Some XV/XVI Century Italian Textiles by Scanning Electron Microscopy-Energy Dispersive X-Ray Spectrometry', in *Materials Issues in Art and Archaeology III* (San Francisco, California: Materials Research Society).

13. Hardin, I. R. and F. J. Duffield (1986): 'Characterization of Metallic Yarns in Historic Persian Textiles by Microanalysis', in *Historic Textile and Paper Materials*, ACS Symposium Series 212 (American Chemical Society).

14. Darrah, J. A. (1987): 'Metal Threads and Filaments', in *Jubilee Conservation Conference; Recent Advances in the Conservation and Analysis of Artefacts* (University of London Institute of Archaeology: Summer School Press), pp. 211-22.

15. Indictor, N., *et al.* (1988): 'The Evaluation of Metal Wrappings from Medieval Textiles Using Scanning Electron Microscopy-Energy Dispersive X-Ray Spectrometry', in *Textile History*, 19(1), pp. 3-19.

16. Indictor, N., *et al.* (1988): 'Metal Threads Made of Proteinaceous Substrates Examined by Scanning Electron Microscopy-Energy Dispersive X-Ray Spectrometry', in *Studies in Conservation*, 34, pp. 171-82.

17. Montegut, D., *et al.* (1996): 'Technical Examination of Metal Threads in Some Indonesian Textiles of West Sumatra', *Textile History*, 27(1), pp. 101-114.

18. Járó, M., Toth, A. and E. Gondar (1990): 'Determination of the Manufacturing Technique of a 10th Century Metal Thread', in *Preprints of ICOM Committee for Conservation*, 9th Triennial meeting (Dresden), pp. 299-301.

19. Járó, M., Gondar, E. and A. Toth (1993): 'Technical Revolutions in Producing Gold Threads Used for European Textile Decoration', in *Outils et ateliers d'orfèvres des temps anciens* (Château de Sait-Germain-el-Laye: Société des Amis du Musée des Antiquités Nationales), pp. 119.

20. Darrah, J. A. (1989): 'The Microscopical and Analytical Examination of Three Types of Metal Thread', in *International Restorer Seminar* (Veszprem, Hungary: National Centre of Museums), pp. 53-63.

21. Oddy, W. A. (1977): 'The Production of Gold Wire in Antiquity. Hand-Making Methods before the Introduction of the Draw-Plate', in *Gold Bulletin*, 10(3), pp. 79-87.

22. Járó, M., Gondar, E. and A. Toth (1990): 'Reconstruction of Gilding Techniques used for Medieval Membrane Threads in Museum Textiles', in *Archeometry '90* (Basel: Birkhaeuser Verlag), pp. 317-25.

23. Járó, M. and A. Toth (1991): 'Scientific Identification of European Metal Thread Manufacturing Techniques of the 17th-19th centuries', in *Endeavour* (UK), 15(4), pp. 175-84.

24. Ferreira, E. S. B. (2002): 'New Approaches towards the identification of yellow dyes in ancient textiles', *PhD Thesis* (University of Edinburgh); Feller, R. L. (1994): *Accelerated Aging: Photochemical and*

Thermal Aspects (Marina del Rey: Getty Conservation Institute).

25. Ferreira, E. S. B. (2002): ibid.
26. Peggie, D. (2006): 'The Development and Application of Analytical Methods for the Identification of Dyes on Historical Textiles', *PhD Thesis* (University of Edinburgh).
27. Ferreira, E. S. B. (2002): ibid.
28. Ferreira, E. S. B., Quye, A., Hulme, A. N., H. McNab (2003): 'LC-Ion Trap MS and PDA-HPLC – Complementary Techniques in the Analysis of Flavonoid Dyes in Historical Textiles: The Case Study of an 18th Century Herald's Tabard', in *Dyes in History and Archaeology*, vol. 19, pp. 13-18.
–   Petroviciu I. and J. Wouters (2002): 'Analysis of Natural Dyes from Romanian 19th- and 20th-century Ethnographical Textiles by DAD-HPLC', in *Dyes in History and Archaeology*, v. 18, pp. 57-62.
–   Trojanowicz, M., Orska-Gawry, Ê. J., Surowiec, I., Szostek, B., Urbaniak-Walczak, K., Kehl, J., M. Wrobel (2004): 'Chromatographic Investigation of Dyes Extracted from Coptic Textiles from the National Museum in Warsaw', in *Studies in Conservation*, vol. 49, pp. 115-30.
29. BS EN ISO 13934-1:1999.
30. Robinet, L. and D. A. Thickett (2003): 'New Methodology for Accelerated Corrosion testing', in *Studies in Conservation*, vol. 48, pp. 263-68.
31. Vanden Berghe I. and J. Wouters (2005): 'Identification and condition evaluation of deteriorated protein fibres at the sub-microgram level by calibrated amino acid analysis', in *Scientific Analysis of Ancient and Historic Textiles: Informing Preservation, Display and Interpretation Postprints* (London: Archetype), pp. 151-58.
32. Hallett, K. and D. Howell (2005): 'Size exclusion chromatography as a tool for monitoring silk degradation in historic tapestries', in *Scientific Analysis of Ancient and Historic Textiles: Informing Preservation, Display and Interpretation Postprints* (London: Archetype), pp. 143-50.
–   Hallett, K. and D. Howell (2005): 'Size exclusion chromatography of silk – inferring the tensile strength and assessing the condition of historic tapestries', in *Preprints of ICOM Committee for Conservation*, 14th Triennial meeting (The Hague, Netherlands), 12-16 September 2005, pp. 911-19.
33. Carr, C. M. and D. M. Lewis (1993): 'An FTIR Spectroscopic Study of the Photodegradation and thermal degradation of wool', in *Journal of Society of Dyers and Colourists*, vol. 109, pp. 21-24.
–   Kellner, R., Mermet, J.-M., Otto, M. and H. M. Widmer (eds) (1998): 'Infrared and Raman Spectroscopy',

in *Analytical Chemistry* (Weinheim: Wiley-VCH Verlag GmbH), pp. 541-65.
34. Rouessac, F. and A. Rouessac (2000): *Chemical Analysis, Modern Instrumentation Methods and Techniques* (John Wiley & Sons Ltd), pp. 161-87.
35. Carr and Lewis (1993): ibid.
36. Goldstein, J. I., Newbury, D. E., Echlin, P., Joy, D. C., Fiori, C. and E. Lifshin (1981): *Scanning Electron Microscopy and X-Ray Microanalysis* (New York, London: Plenum Press).
37. Briggs, D. (1998): *Surface Analysis of Polymers by XPS and Static SIMS* (Cambridge: Cambridge University Press), pp. 14-47.
–   Moulder, J. F., Stickle, W. F., Sobol, P. E. and K. D. Bomben (1992 and 1995): *Handbook of X-ray Photo-electron Spectroscopy* (Eden Prairie, Minnesota: Physical Electronics, Inc.), pp. 9-33, 128.
–   Watts, F. J. (1990): *An Introduction to Surface Analysis by Electron Spectroscopy* (Oxford University Press; Royal Microscopical Society), pp. 1-23.
38. Briggs, D., Brown, A. and J. C. Vickerman (1989): *Handbook of Static Secondary Ion Mass Spectroscopy* (John Wiley & Sons), pp. 3-15.
–   Cherepin, V. T. (1987): *Secondary Ion Mass Spectroscopy of Solid Surfaces* (Utrecht: VNU Science Press BV), pp. 1-92.
–   Vickerman, J. C., Brown, A. and N. M. Reed (eds) (1989): 'Secondary Ion Mass Spectroscopy. Principles and Applications', in *The International Series of Monographs on Chemistry* (Oxford: Clarendon Press), p. 22.
39. Luo, M, Cui, G. and B. Rigg (2001): 'The development of the CIE 2000 colour-difference formula: CIEDE2000', in *Color Research and Application*, vol. 26, pp. 340-50.
40. Odlyha, M., Wang, Q., Foster, G. M., de Groot, J., Horton, M. and L. Bozec (2005): 'Thermal Analysis of Model and Historic Tapestries', *Journal of Thermal Analysis and Calorimetry*, v. 82(3), pp. 627-36.
41. Hacke (2006): ibid.
42. Vanden Berghe and Wouters (2005): ibid.
43. Peggie (2006): ibid.
44. Wouters, J. and A. Verhecken (1989): 'The scale insect dyes (Homoptera: Coccoidea). Species recognition by HPLC and Diode-Array analysis of the dyestuff', in *Annales Soc. Entomologique France*, (N.S.) 25(4), p. 393.
45. Peggie, D. A., Hulme, A. N., McNab, H. and A. Quye (2008): 'Towards the identification of characteristic minor components from textiles dyed with weld (*Reseda luteola L.*) and those dyed with Mexican cochineal (*Dactylopius coccus Costa*)', in *Microchimica Acta*, vol. 162(3-4), pp. 371-80.

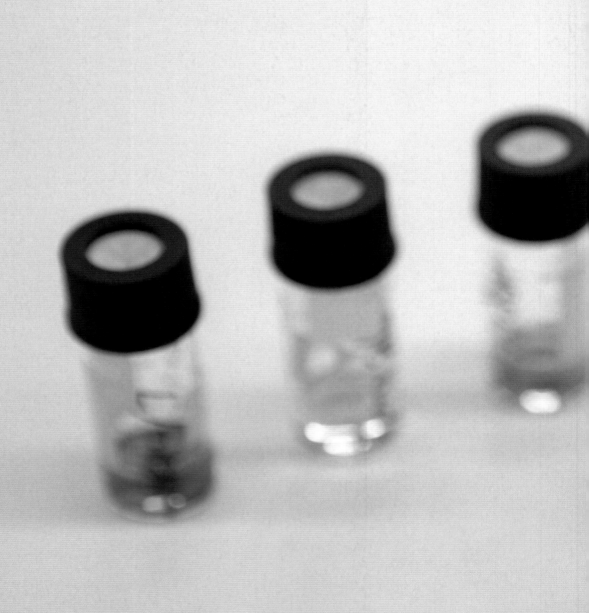

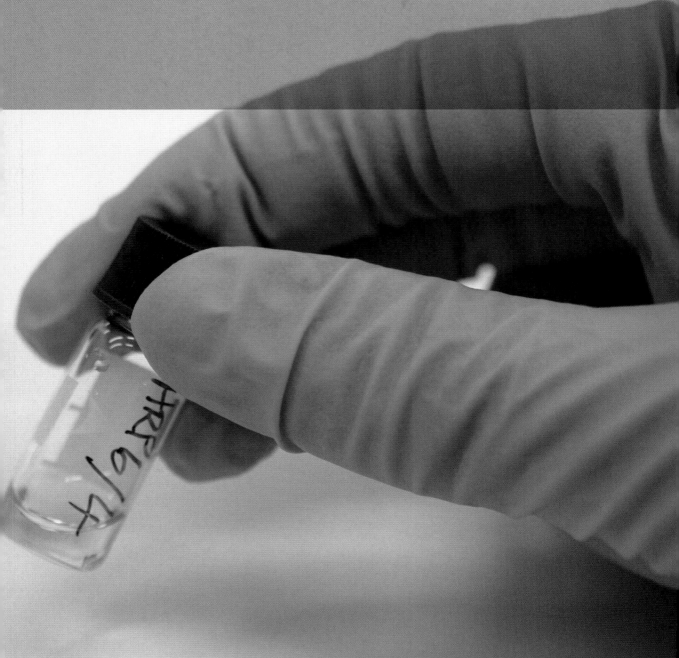

CHAPTER 4

Results

Marei Hacke, Kathryn Hallett, David Peggie,
Anita Quye and Ina Vanden Berghe

Preparing to analyse
the historical tapestries

BEFORE analysing selected historical samples, the researchers
had honed and compared their analytical methods by using
model tapestries to simulate yet simplify the complex structure of
the originals (see chapter 3). From this we understood better how the
strength of wool and silk yarns was influenced by ageing processes
that shortened the lengths of their chemical (protein) chains, and in
turn how much these proteins were likely to change in fibres exposed
for centuries to glass-filtered daylight as well as atmospheric oxygen
and water. We had also discovered how much the dyeing process
influenced the original strength of the yarns when the tapestries
were made. Blue woad imparted an almost protective effect on both
wool and silk, in contrast to the weakening effect of dyeing silk red
with a commonly-used combination of cochineal, copper, iron and
oak galls.

   Drawing on the above, the research team confidently entered the
next phase of the project – to analyse and interpret materials from
the historical tapestries. The questions being addressed all related to
identifying meaningful markers of damage. How strong were the
tapestries? Did different histories, such as place and period of manufacture, use and care, have a detectable effect on current strength?
Could their condition be ranked? What could be predicted for future
changes? From the range of analytical tools tested on the models, the
most useful for discovering markers of damage in the historical tapestries appeared to be: amino acid measurements by HPLC, ATR-
FTIR and XPS; protein chain lengths by average molecular weight
distribution using SEC; and dye identification by PDA-HPLC and
LC-MS (see chapter 3 and appendix 1). Metal threads hold particular
importance for historical tapestry studies and would be examined
for a comparative study of physical appearance and construction,

as well as corrosion, by applying the well-established high magnification method of SEM.

Seventeen of some of the world's exceptionally important European tapestries were chosen from the Belgian cathedrals of Bruges and Tournai [TC], the Royal Museum of Art and History in Brussels [RMAH], the Royal Collections at Hampton Court Palace in London [HCP] and the Royal Palace, Madrid [PRM]. Selection criteria included the quality of manufacture; completeness of historical record for purchase, use and care; and interconnections such as analogous copies of each other (see chapter 2). Taking samples required careful planning, not only to be granted access to the priceless textiles, but also to maximise the limited time spent at each location. Three separate sampling campaigns, lasting two to three full days, were arranged where, guided by conservators and curators, the scientists selected and recorded adequate lengths of loose yarns and metal threads from the reverse of each tapestry before carefully removing them with needlework scissors and storing them in meticulously-labelled inert sample containers. On return to the labs, the samples (averaging 40 per tapestry) were sequentially distributed. The process and lessons learned are detailed in chapter 5.

The many painstaking and physically-demanding hours of concentrated team effort to sample the tapestries did not go unrewarded. Memorable occasions included an honoured tour of the breathtaking Royal Apartments in the Royal Palace, Madrid, rarely seen by the public; working in the Tournai Cathedral vestry on a tapestry normally housed in the treasure room while large-scale building conservation work carried on around us; and holding a project meeting in Katherine of Aragon's apartment

FIGURE 4.1 (pages 74-75, and opposite)

Silk samples dissolved in a concentrated salt solution prior to size exclusion chromatography analysis.
(© Historic Royal Palaces)

FIGURE 4.2 (above)

Accurately measuring the co-ordinates of a sample location on a tapestry is a vital part of the research documentation.
(© MODHT Project)

FIGURE 4.3 (below)

Carefully selecting a sample for analysis after accurately measuring the co-ordinates of its location on the tapestry.
(© MODHT Project)

FIGURE 4.4

The accurate and delicate tools used by
conservators to remove samples from a tapestry
are similar to those wielded by a surgeon.
(© Historic Royal Palaces)

at Hampton Court Palace. Many of the tapestries researched have been seen by tens of thousands of visitors to these famous historical sites, which made the project team feel privileged to work on such important and well known works of textile art.

From model to historical tapestries

Each scientific technique tested on the models provided a different way of representing fibre degradation. Amino acid analysis was successful in measuring oxidation and hydrolysis occurring at the molecular level, by comparing how the relative proportions of amino acids changed. This was compared to ATR-FTIR data, which measured the amount of oxidation to the amino acid cystine, con-

verting it to cysteic acid. Another way of expressing this degradation mechanism was defined using XPS, which provided the percentage of oxidised sulfur as a marker of amino acid oxidation and cysteic acid formation. Because XPS was so surface-sensitive compared to the other techniques, it offered potential for detecting early-warning markers.

Size exclusion chromatography provided the next level of information by expressing the amount of chain scission which had occurred through degradation. Chain scission is the breaking up of the protein chains into shorter lengths and is directly related to the tensile strength of the polymer. This correlation was demonstrated with the model tapestries. While not intended to be a direct marker of damage, the tensile strength results provided the final step in the diagnostic sequence for predicting the ability of a tapestry to bear its own weight, and thus to be displayed.

Each technique provided complementary information about the condition of the fibres, but also helped to uncover the cause of the decay: for example, where the dyestuff or mordant was shown to enhance the degradation of the model samples. The research directed at understanding the dyestuffs revealed dye breakdown products which enabled the identification of aged samples that would previously have been unknown. The link established between dye/mordant and degradation meant that a full condition assessment benefits from including the manufacture materials and processes.

The scientific results are summarised below. More detailed, technical results are in the publications referenced at the end of this chapter, especially the doctoral research theses of David Peggie (dye analysis and degradation)[1] and Marei Hacke (fibre surface analysis and metal threads).[2]

Historical sample results

Dyes

The number of coloured yarns analysed by PDA-HPLC for dye identification approached 500,[3] of which approximately half were visibly yellow and green. Irrespective of weaving centre or manufacturing date within the 300-year span of interest, the natural yellow dye sources were consistently found to be weld and dyer's greenweed, both native to Europe at the time. A general trend appeared for the preference of one dye over another for a fibre type – typically dyer's greenweed (often in combination with other dyes) for silk and weld for wool.

Damage was evident in the dyestuffs, even in samples taken from the backs of historic tapestries. PDA-HPLC analysis detected dye degradation products (the chemical fragments which appear when the original dye molecules have broken down) in many samples. Where the dyes were formed from chemically similar components, the dye degradation products tended to be similar – as found with weld and dyer's greenweed, for example.

Areas of restoration obvious to the trained eyes of conservators were sampled. As expected, most proved to be post mid-nineteenth century, based on the synthetic dyes present. Evidence of older repairs was revealed in five samples from two tapestries by the detection of the yellow dye, old fustic. Although naturally-derived, this North American dye was introduced to Europe long after the tapestries were reliably recorded as being made, thus indicating repairs. The repair yarns were also relatively stronger than the original tapestry.

All yellow silk cores of the 25 metal threads analysed from six tapestries [PNM1, PNM2, PNM5, BXL2, BXL4 and HRP2; see chapter 2 for code definitions] confirmed the consistent use of young fustic. The metallic strips wound around them adequately protected the dyed silk threads from damaging light that would have otherwise caused the colour to fade. This also enabled the makers to combine the yellow with an equally light-sensitive red dye – brazilwood – to colour match the core yarns closely and cheaply with their gilded outer metal. Indeed, all the fibres dyed with this combination were identified from gilded metal threads, thus supporting this hypothesis.

Of the limited red sources available to the dyers, the European native plant dye madder appeared to be the most popular, used alone and in combination with additional dyes like yellow flavonoid plant dyes, blue indigoid dyes, and, occasionally, red brazilwood. Several yarns had been dyed with Mexican cochineal which was imported into Europe

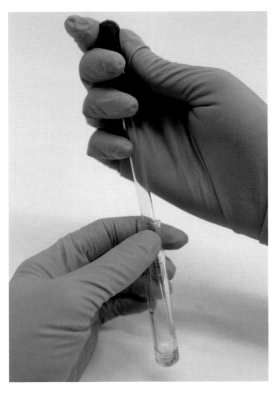

FIGURE 4.5

Samples were carefully prepared for chromatographic analyses by dissolving the fibre in a solvent or salt solution. (© Historic Royal Palaces)

Fibres

At the project outset, the researchers had concerns that yarns sampled from the unexposed back of tapestries would not prove appropriate for markers of damage. Because faded colours are, regrettably, a notable feature of most historic tapestries, light is perceived to be the most damaging environmental factor, and the yarns analysed had been protected from direct exposure. The colours on the reverse of the tapestries were outstandingly bright, leaving no doubt to the quality of artistic detail, the artisan skill of their makers, and their magnificence when in full, undamaged glory. Another area of concern was whether the accelerated ageing regimes would realistically model the course of natural ageing that the tapestries had undergone, or perhaps would even be too harsh.

It was therefore greatly encouraging for viable practical application of the research, and perhaps somewhat surprising, for the amino acid analysis to reveal that the historic samples from the protected side of tapestries showed as much, if not more, degradation than predicted from the model studies. This was supported by results from the average molecular weight analysis of silk yarns which showed that the historic samples were, again, considerably more degraded than had been expected compared to the models. This indicates that light may not be the only important degradation factor over time periods of several hundred years. As predicted from the models, the blue historical fibres identified as indigoid dyed (woad or indigo) generally measured the highest average molecular weight, i.e. were the least damaged.

A system of ranking damage within each tapestry was attempted, but the high level of

from 1518,[4] earlier than the manufacturing date for four of the five tapestries where cochineal had been used, so these yarns were likely to be original. For the fifth tapestry, *Christ before Pilate* [BXL2], made at an earlier date in Brussels, the two cochineal-dyed yarns indicated restorative work. Unlike the yellow dyes, no correlation was found between the yarn type and the red dye used. Blue and blue-containing dyes were invariably the chemically indistinguishable indigoid dyes, woad and indigo.

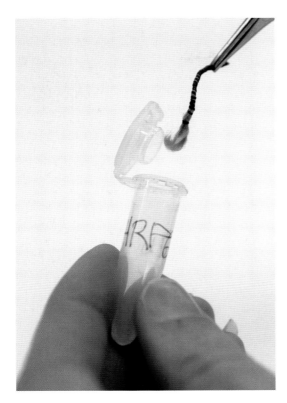

higher than statistically ideal, it enabled upper and lower extremes to be evaluated, taking into account the experimental error, and yielded interesting information. The Bruges *Verdure with Coat of Arms of Brugse Vrije* [fragments BRU1] was consistently and surprisingly found to have the highest average molecular weight, whereas the Spanish *Tobias presents Raphael to his Father* [PNM7] recorded the lowest average molecular weight. Thus it could be argued that the Bruges tapestry was less damaged and stronger than the Spanish one.

The viability of this type of assessment was supported by the analysis of the three Hampton Court Palace tapestries, where it was possible to correlate the measured properties with the conservators' condition assessments. One of the tapestries [HRP3, *Triumph of Death over Chastity*] was assessed visually to be in the worst condition, and the high level of degradation was confirmed by analysis of average molecular weight and amino acids, and also by ATR-FTIR. The implication is that scientific analysis could feasibly aid decisions based on whether it would be safer to handle and display one tapestry compared to another.[5]

There did not seem to be any relationship between the location of the sample from across the reverse of a tapestry (e.g. top, middle, bottom edge) and the chemical markers of damage values. Five wool samples taken as a special privilege from the front side of one historic tapestry, unsurprisingly, showed even more degradation than the ones taken from the backs. If a combination of iron and copper sulfate with oak galls had been originally used for black, the yarns were no longer evident in the historic tapestries, probably because they had already degraded. Thus it was not possible to evaluate the effect of iron and copper on the fibre degradation

variation made it difficult from a simple comparative assessment. After looking at the data gathered from the model tapestries, it was apparent that dyeing and other manufacture processes were responsible for some measurable differences, in addition to other causes such as inconspicuous historic restoration.

In response to this, an attempt was made to compare 'like for like' between tapestries by only comparing data from any yarns which had been dyed with the same dyestuff. Silk yarns dyed yellow and green with dyer's greenweed were chosen because there were more of these than the other fibre-dye combinations. Although variation was still

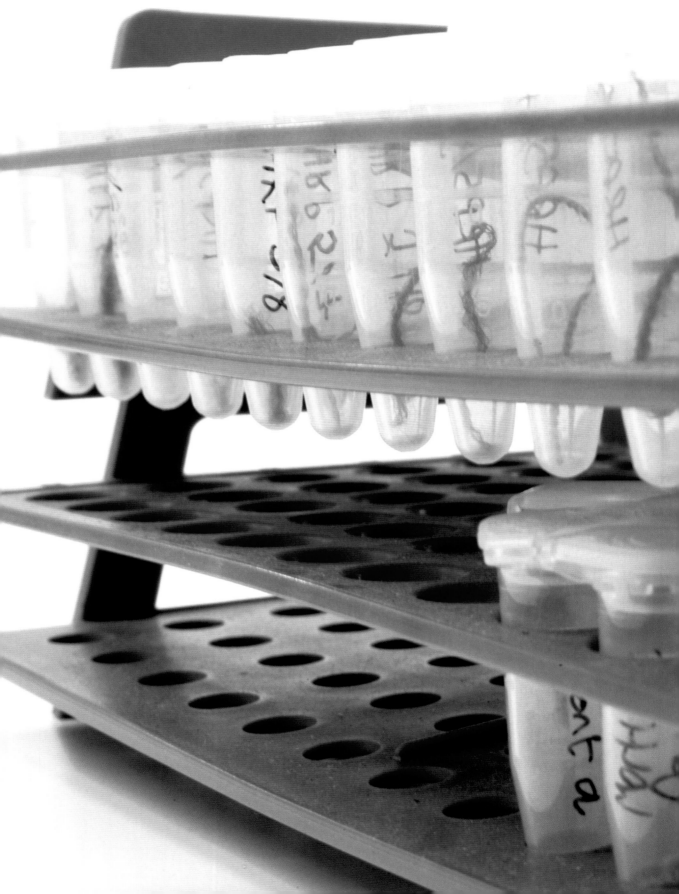

by measuring the formation of cysteic acid, as found in the model samples [chapter 3]. Wool threads with synthetic dyes indicated restoration from the last quarter of the 19th century onwards and were, as expected, in a much less degraded state than an original tapestry fibre.

Silk core yarns of metal threads from the historic tapestries were also analysed by amino acid analysis. The selection of these silks was based on the grouping of the metal threads: silver threads, gilt silver threads and a third group of highly corroded gilt silver threads. No significant difference could be seen between the silk core yarns from metal threads and the other historic silk samples. In fact, in one tapestry the silk core yarns were actually less degraded than the silk samples, perhaps due to less exposure to light. There was also no apparent difference in fibre degradation relating to the composition of the metal strip wrapped around the core yarn, regardless of whether the metal strip was silver or gilt, corroded or not.

Surface analysis

Chemical

Fibre surfaces yielded useful information about the chemical and physical state of the yarns, especially when examined by XPS, which detected increased oxidised sulfur levels in wool as the amino acid cystine converted to cysteic acid. XPS also revealed a greater loss of nitrogen-containing compounds from historical tapestries compared to model ones, indicating that real-time ageing effects were more aggressive than predicted, and so was considered a promising tapestry damage assessment tool. With further development, SIMS [chapter 3], if available, could be another good screening method for cysteic acid because it causes minimal sample damage. ATR-FTIR for model and historical woollen threads gives a rapid non-destructive method for assessing extent of damage in terms of the cysteic acid marker. Comparison with light aged model wool samples gives an estimate of the severity of damage.

Physical

Although the samples taken from the back of the historical tapestries were found to be chemically much more degraded that the model fibres, their magnified physical appearance by SEM [chapter 3] was generally indistinguishable, with their range of fracture types being similar for both wool and silk. A small number of wool yarns from reverse-side sampling showed transverse cracks and either flaking or complete lost of the cuticles, similar to the few samples taken from the front of tapestries which had been more exposed to light. Dyeing seemed to damage silk surfaces, manifested as thin strips peeling off the otherwise smooth surface and longitudinal cracks, with transverse cracks and brittle breaks observed on historic silk only. This was unexpected. While interesting and informative, SEM analysis was found to be too subjective as an accurate damage assessment tool for historic fibres because the observations for unaged, model and historic fibres were indistinguishable [see Figures 4.8-10].

FIGURE 4.7

Fibre samples were stored in carefully labelled vials and cross-checked against sampling records to avoid contamination or loss. (© Historic Royal Palaces)

Investigations of the metal threads

Precious metal threads were often reserved for tapestries of the highest quality and the individual threads' fineness and intricacy of structure were intriguing. Sadly today the tarnished metals often blemish the tapestries' appearance, but the influence of the organic construction materials on the corrosion of the inorganic metals had not been systematically studied before the project. Through MODHT it was possible to assess nearly 200 metal threads of similar age and application from the tapestries *Christ before Pilate* [BXL2] (Royal Museum of Art and History, Brussels); *The Meeting of Abraham and Melchizedek* (Hampton Court Palace, London) (which is not analysed elsewhere in MODHT); and *Daedalus and Icarus*, *Jupiter and Ganymede* and *Neoptolemus and Polyxena* which belong to the 'Fables of Ovid' tapestry series (from the Royal Palace, Madrid) [PNM1, PNM2 AND PNM5]. Although the tapestries were all woven in Belgium in the 16th century, the metal threads showed a range of structural and damage differences.

Optical microscopy is typically used when studying historic objects to examine the overall appearance of samples under lower magnification (typically from x 10 to x 400) before moving on to more expensive specialist equipment. In studying the metal threads, optical microscopy, followed by SEM-EDX and SIMS, were used to look at dimensional features and alloy composition to find out more about the historic manufacturing techniques.[6]

All the metal thread samples consisted of solid metal filaments wound around a yarn core of silk that was either white or light yellow for silver threads and darker yellow

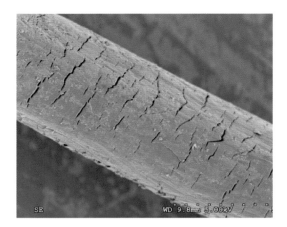

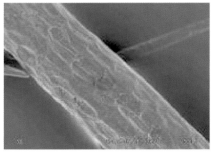

FIGURES 4.8-10

These images illustrate the most advanced damage observed – transverse cracking and loss of cuticles from wool fibres. However, many historic wool fibres look the same as unaged fibres, meaning that SEM examination can be misleading.
(Figs 4.8-10 © University of Manchester)

84

shades for gilt threads, the exception being the number of restoration threads which had cotton core fibres. Historical core yarns typically exhibited a low twist in the opposite direction to the metal filament. Double and even triple wrappings of the highest quality precious metal threads, sometimes concentrated at eye-level on the hanging tapestries, showed unusual examples of overt wealth in four out of the five tapestries studied [see Figures 4.11-12]. Threads of the smallest diameter seemed the most intricate in manufacture; extremely fine and so tightly wrapped that the silk core was hardly visible.

The interpretation of metal thread images allowed the identification of trends between metal thread dimensions, indicating that manufacturers chose wider filaments for the spinning of coarser metal threads and the finest filaments for the spinning of threads with the smallest diameter and narrow winding. The relative amounts of coarse and fine metal threads and the number of double and triple wrapped threads observed in the investigated tapestries suggested a deliberate choice of the highest quality metal threads in

the Spanish 'Fables of Ovid' tapestries [PNM2 and PNM5], while the varying levels of corrosion between the different tapestries signify their display and storage histories.

Establishing the manufacturing technique was possible by SEM analysis of the edges of the metal threads.[7] Sharp angles, with tool marks left from cutting, indicate 'beaten and cut' threads where a block of silver was gilt on one side and beaten into a thin sheet before cutting into strips for winding around a yarn core. In contrast, smooth and round filament edges and longitudinal striations are characteristic for 'cast, drawn and rolled' threads, meaning rods of cast silver were surface gilt, drawn into thin wire and rolled to produce a flattened filament for winding around the core fibres. Caution was, however, raised by SEM analysis of model metal threads produced from flattened wires because their edges were also often rough with sharp angles, and hence misleading. It was concluded that determination of the manufacturing technique must include analysis of the metal filaments' exterior and interior sides to ascertain single- or double-

FIGURE 4.11

Detail of multi-wrapped metal thread from *The Meeting of Abraham and Melchizedek*, Hampton Court Palace [no MODHT code]. (© University of Manchester)

FIGURE 4.12

Magnified detail of a multi-wrapped metal thread from *Daedalus and Icarus* [PNM1]. (© University of Manchester)

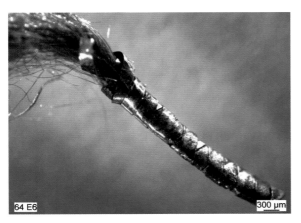

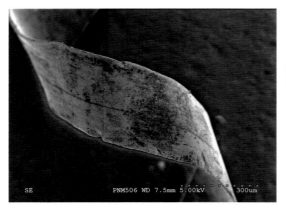

FIGURE 4.13

SEM micrograph of metal thread from *Neoptomelus and Polyxena* [PMN5] showing longitudinal striation. (© University of Manchester)

FIGURE 4.14

SEM micrograph of metal thread from *Neoptomelus and Polyxena* [PMN5]. (© University of Manchester)

sided gilding, indicative of 'beaten and cut' or 'cast, drawn and rolled' manufacture respectively.

'Beaten and cut' metal threads of solid gold may have been manufactured since the times of ancient Egypt and samples of silver gilt 'beaten and cut' threads appeared from the 10th century onwards.[8] In comparison, the 'cast, drawn and rolled' method is a relatively modern production pathway with the changeover from 'beaten and cut' threads occurring between the late 15th or 16th century to the 17th century.[9] The five tapestries with metal threads analysed in this project were produced in Brussels in the first half of the 16th century: *Christ before Pilate* [1520, BXL2], *The Meeting of Abraham and Melchizedek* [1540, no code] and the 'Fables of Ovid' series [1545, PNM1, 2 and 5].

SEM-EDX results show that all but one of the analysed metal threads were gilt on one side only, suggesting the 'beaten and cut' manufacturing route. One sample from the *Christ before Pilate* tapestry showed some gold on the interior of the metal filament; however, the early production date of the tapestry and the similarity with EDX results

of a restoration thread suggested that this particular sample was also a restoration thread and thus a later inclusion in the tapestry. Other restoration threads were of an even later date, with mercerized cotton core fibres and a Pinchbeck brass filament.

Cross sectional analyses of metal threads showed the silver-copper bulk as a single phase alloy which may have been deliberately achieved to retain the metal's relative flexibility. The cross-sections also showed the presence of pores in the alloy which were stretched longitudinally parallel to the axis of the filaments, suggesting that the metals were rolled during manufacturing. This was supported by the longitudinal striations on the surface of a metal filament [see Figures 4.13, 14]. Pores on the edges of the filaments showed signs of compression due to cutting from the non-gilt side (interior) to the gilt side (exterior) [see Figure 4.15]. This combination of rolling and cutting for the manufacture of metal threads contributes new information to the common hypotheses of manufacturing routes being divided into 'beaten and cut' and 'cast, drawn and rolled'.

Surface analysis using SIMS depth profiles, and SEM of cross sections indicated gold layer thicknesses of less than 0.5 µm (smaller than one-thousandth of a millimetre). These extremely thin gold layers are consistent with other recent studies on metal threads which revealed thinner gold layers than it was previously thought possible to achieve.[10] When looking at the cross-sections using the very high magnification of the SEM, a clear distinction between the gold layers and the silver-copper bulk was observed. In addition, the gold layers were splitting apart in some places while overlapping gold leaves were clearly seen in others. All of these observations suggest that the leaf gilding technique was used.

Metal thread corrosion products were analysed using surface analysis techniques (SEM-EDX and XPS) and compared to the accelerated tarnishing tests carried out using model tapestries (chapter 3), which aimed to establish whether the breakdown of differently dyed wool and silk influenced the formation and chemistry of corrosion compounds. Crystals, mainly rounded, were observed on the surfaces of the metal filaments, and the corrosion grew as layers with varying compositions. Most samples had a layer rich in silver and sulfur content detaching from a layer containing copper and carbon [see Figure 4.16]. In some places the metal filament had even disintegrated because the corrosion had 'tunnelled' into the bulk. Precise identification of the corrosion products on the metal threads was achieved using X-ray diffraction (XRD). In a XRD machine an X-ray beam is aimed at the sample, which causes the beam to be scattered into characteristic patterns for the crystalline compounds present. Due to the small sample dimensions, XRD analysis of metal threads was difficult and often failed. For those metal threads where XRD patterns

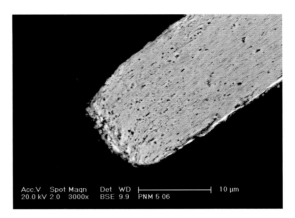

FIGURE 4.15

SEM micrograph of a cross-section through a metal thread from *Neoptomelus and Polyxena* [PNM5], showing compression towards the gilt side.
(© University of Manchester)

were successfully obtained, the minerals acanthite (silver sulfide) and chlorargyrite (silver chloride) were identified.

Conclusion

The collective results from the scientific teams, combined with curatorial and conservation expertise, established that samples taken from the reverse of tapestries provided valuable condition-related information. The research also revealed skilled craftsmanship from five hundred years ago, especially in the making of metal threads.

The practical aspects of the project were challenging – the team worked hard to refine methodologies to make full use of a limited precious resource, and this process is described in chapter 5. As a result, the potential of scientific data for condition assessment, in combination with conservator assessment, was evaluated in more detail than previously possible. The results largely matched and confirmed the hypotheses put forward on the basis of the model tapestry analysis, but

PNM2-19   300 µm

FIGURE 4.16

Micrograph showing typical black corrosion (silver sulfide) on a gilt metal thread, from *Jupiter and Ganymede* [PNM2]. (© University of Manchester)

there were a few surprises too – especially the advanced level of degradation measured in fibres from the reverse of historic tapestries, even though the dyestuffs still retained their bright colours.

Specific markers have been established that can function as early warning indicators for the chemical degradation of both wool and silk fibres. This opens the door to different practical applications making it possible to follow the degradation of a tapestry over a large time span, or to compare the condition of different tapestries at one time.

References

1. Peggie, D. (2006): 'The Development and Application of Analytical Methods for the Identification of Dyes on Historical Textiles', PhD Thesis (University of Edinburgh).
2. Hacke, A-M. (2006): 'Investigation into the Nature and Ageing of Tapestry Materials', PhD Thesis (University of Manchester).
3. Ferreira, E. S. B., Hulme, A. N., McNab H. and A. Quye (2004): 'The natural constituents of historical textile dyes', *Chemical Society Reviews*, v. 33, pp. 329-36.
   – Peggie, D. A., Hulme, A. N., McNab, H. and A. Quye (in press): 'The chemical characterisation of aged and unaged fibre samples dyed with sawwort (*Serratula tinctoria*) using PDA HPLC and HPLC ESI MS', in *Dyes in History and Archaeology*, vol. 22.

   – Hulme, A. N., McNab, H., Peggie, D. A. and A. Quye (2005): 'The application of liquid chromatography-mass spectrometry and accelerated light ageing for the analytical identification of yellow flavonoid dyes in historical tapestries', in *Scientific Analysis of Ancient and Historic Textiles: Informing Preservation, Display and Interpretation*, AHRB Research Centre for Textile Conservation and Textile Studies First Annual Conference, 13-15 July 2004 (Textile Conservation Centre, Winchester Campus, University of Southampton, UK), pp. 208-16.
   – Hulme, A. N., McNab, H., Peggie, D. A. and A. Quye (2005): 'Negative ion electrospray mass spectrometry of neoflavonoids', in *Phytochemistry*, vol. 66(23), pp. 2766-70.
   – Hulme, A. N., McNab, H., Peggie, D. A., Quye, A., Vanden Berghe, I. and J. Wouters (2005): 'The analytical characterisation of the main component found in logwood dyed textile samples after hydrochloric acid extraction', in *Preprints of ICOM Committee for Conservation*, 14th Triennial meeting (The Hague, Netherlands), 12-16 September 2005, pp. 783-88.
   – Peggie, D. A., Hulme, A. N., McNab, H. and A. Quye (2008): 'Towards the identification of characteristic minor components from textiles dyed with weld (Reseda luteola L.) and those dyed with Mexican cochineal (Dactylopius coccus Costa)', *Microchimica Picta*, 162, pp. 371-80.
4. Hofenk de Graff, J. (2004): *The colourful past: Origins, chemistry and identification of natural dyestuffs*, first edition (Abegg-Stiftung and Archetype Publications Ltd).
5. Hallett, K. and D. Howell (2005): 'Size exclusion chromatography as a tool for monitoring silk degradation in historic tapestries', in *Scientific Analysis of Ancient and Historic Textiles: Inform-*

ing Preservation, Display and Interpretation, AHRB Research Centre for Textile Conservation and Textile Studies First Annual Conference, 13-15 July 2004 (Textile Conservation Centre, Winchester Campus, University of Southampton, UK), pp. 143-50.

—   Hallett, K. and D. Howell (2005): 'Size exclusion chromatography of silk – inferring the tensile strength and assessing the condition of historic tapestries', in *Preprints of ICOM Committee for Conservation*, 14th Triennial meeting (The Hague, Netherlands),12-16 September 2005, pp. 911-19.

—   Odlyha, M., Wang, Q., Foster, G. M., de Groot, J., Horton, M. and L. Bozec (2005): 'Monitoring of damage to historic tapestries: The application of dynamic mechanical thermal analysis to model and historic tapestries', in *Scientific Analysis of Ancient and Historic Textiles: Informing Preservation, Display and Interpretation*, AHRB Research Centre for Textile Conservation and Textile Studies First Annual Conference, 13-15 July 2004 (Textile Conservation Centre, Winchester Campus, University of Southampton, UK), pp. 126-36.

—   Odlyha, M., Theodorakopoulos, C. and R. Campana (2007): 'Studies on Woollen Threads from Historical tapestries', in *AUTEX Research Journal*, vol. 7(1), March 2007, pp. 9-18.

—   Odlyha, M. (2003): 'The applications of thermo-analytical techniques to the preservation of art and archaeological objects', in *Handbook of Thermal Analysis and Calorimetry* (Elsevier), vol. 2, ch. 2, pp. 47-96.

—   Vanden Berghe, I. and J. Wouters (2005): 'Identification and condition evaluation of protein fibres at the sub-microgram level by calibrated amino-acid analysis', in *Scientific Analysis of Ancient and Historic Textiles: Informing Preservation, Display and Interpretation*, AHRB Research Centre for Textile Conservation and Textile Studies First Annual Conference, 13-15 July 2004 (Textile Conservation Centre, Winchester Campus, University of Southampton, UK), pp. 151-60.

6. Hacke, A. M., Carr, C. M., Brown, A. and D. Howell (2003): 'Investigation into the nature of metal threads in a renaissance tapestry and the cleaning of tarnished silver by UV/Ozone (UVO) treatment', in *Journal of Materials Science*, v. 38, 3307-14.

—   Hacke, A. M., Carr, C. M. and A. Brown (2005): 'Characterisation of metal threads in Renaissance tapestries', in *Scientific Analysis of Ancient and Historic Textiles: Informing Preservation, Display and Interpretation*, AHRB Research Centre for Textile Conservation and Textile Studies First Annual Conference, 13-15 July 2004 (Textile Conservation

Centre, Winchester Campus, University of Southampton, UK), pp. 71-78.

7. Darrah, J. A. (1987): 'Metal Threads and Filaments', in *Jubilee Conservation Conference; Recent Advances in the Conservation and Analysis of Artefacts* (University of London Institute of Archaeology: Summer School Press), pp. 211-22.

—   Járó, M., Toth, A. and E. Gondar (1990): 'Determination of the Manufacturing Technique of a 10th Century Metal Thread', in *Preprints of ICOM Committee for Conservation*, 9th Triennial meeting (Dresden), pp. 299-301.

—   Járó, M., Gondar, E. and A. Toth (1993): 'Technical Revolutions in Producing Gold Threads Used for European Textile Decoration', in *Outils et ateliers d'orfèvres des temps anciens* (Château de Sait-Germain-el-Laye: Société des Amis du Musée des Antiquités Nationales), pp. 119.

—   Járó, M. (2005): 'The Manufacturing Technique of Gold Threads in the 11th Century Coronation Mantle and some 12-14th Century Coronation Vestments of the Holy Roman Empire', in *Precious Thread: The Manufacture, Trade and Usage of Gold and Silver Yarn in Medieval Society*, Medieval Dress and Textile Society – Autumn Meeting (London: Courtauld Institute of Art).

8. Járó, M., Toth, A. and E. Gondar (1990): ibid.

9. Montegut, D., *et al.* (1992): 'Examination of Metal Threads from some XV/XVI Century Italian Textiles by Scanning Electron Microscopy-Energy Dispersive X-Ray Spectrometry', in *Materials Issues in Art and Archaeology* III (San Francisco, California: Materials Research Society), pp. 309-17.

—   Járó, M., Gondar, E. and A. Toth (1990): 'Reconstruction of Gilding Techniques used for Medieval Membrane Threads in Museum Textiles', in *Archeometry '90* (Basel: Birkhaeuser Verlag), pp. 317-25.

—   Garside, P. (2002): *Investigations of Analytical Techniques for the Characterisation of Natural Textile Fibres towards Informed Conservation* (Southampton: University of Southampton), pp. 1-232 [PhD Thesis].

—   Rogerson, C. (1999): *Report: 15th Century Tapestry Woven Altar Frontal* (Textile Conservation Centre, University of Southampton), pp. 6-26.

10. Enguita, O., *et al.* (2002): 'Characterization of Metal Threads using Differential PIXE Analysis', in *Nuclear Instruments and Methods in Physics Research*, Section B: Beam Interactions with Materials and Atoms, 189(1-4), pp. 328-33.

—   Nord, A. G. and K. Tronner (2000): 'A Note on the Analysis of Gilded Metal Embroidery Threads', in *Studies in Conservation*, vol. 45(4), pp. 274-79.

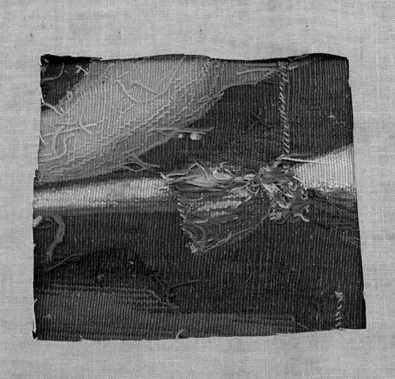

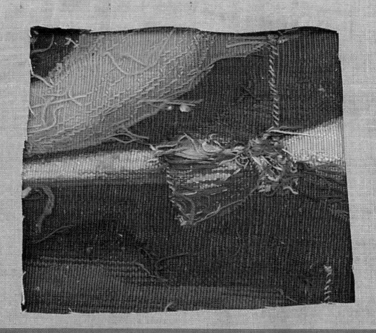

The Project
in Practice

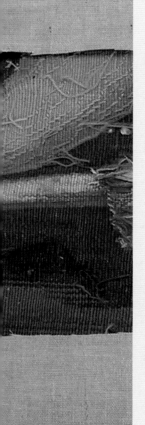

CHAPTER 5

The Project in Practice
A Case Study from Historic Royal Palaces

Kathryn Hallett

THE MODHT project demonstrated that relative damage in tapestries which are centuries old can be measured and interpreted scientifically using protocols acceptable for historical textiles preservation. The project also provided validation of controlled experimentation to model accelerated ageing behaviour for tapestries and created invaluable reference materials for future research projects. To these ends the project has been successful, having fulfilled the researchers' expectations and justified the significant funding and resources invested over three years. Ideas for further scientific investigation of tapestries and application of the project's methodologies to other historical textile studies have also evolved.

The remaining, and ultimate, test of the project's success now rests with acceptance and sustainability of the recommendations by practising professionals, in particular conservators, conservation scientists, curators and collections managers. Feedback from the end-of-project workshop, where our results and findings were presented to target end-users, showed that the project's principles and conclusions were welcomed and encouraged, but the complex science needed to be put into practice to demonstrate that it was a resource-efficient complement to existing approaches. Tina Kane, a textile conservator at the Metropolitan Museum of Art, New York commented:

> The MODHT team presented the results of their investigation at the symposium, at Hampton Court Palace, in 2005. The findings indicated that it was time to re-evaluate some of the more commonly used conservation practices. It is of crucial importance that these findings be published, and made available to a wider audience, so conservators can begin to translate the scientific information into conservation practice.

This publication was inspired by feedback received at the workshop.

In order further to investigate the sometimes difficult translation from research-level analysis to routine testing methods, MODHT researcher Kathryn Hallett (Historic Royal Palaces) arranged a case study with her colleagues at HRP and MODHT partner Ina Vanden Berghe (KIK) to assess the condition of three 17th-century tapestries. Alongside the academic testing of the results were practical queries, particularly exploring realistic achievement with significantly lower levels of funding, sampling opportunities, staff time, and available expertise and analytical techniques. In revising and refining our methodologies over three years, the team developed a protocol designed to be applicable in general operational (non-research level) working as part of the conservation and care of tapestry collections. This chapter describes the practical test case, its methodology of decision-making and working, and outcomes in comparison to the larger research project.

Strategies for using the research in practice

The test case: questions and influencing factors (time, money, people, techniques)

A key aim of MODHT was to deliver a working methodology beyond the framework of a research project which has the time and resources for detailed analytical experimentation. The test case undertaken by the conservation and scientific team at HRP involved three of the collection's 17th-century wool and silk English tapestries, woven in London and at Mortlake, Surrey:

- *The Fleets Drawn up in Lines of Battle* ('Battle of the Solebay' series, 1685, London)
- *Fireships in Action* ('Battle of the Solebay' series, 1685, London)
- *Elymas the Sorcerer struck blind before Sergius Paulus* ('Acts of the Apostles series', 1635, Mortlake, Surrey)

Fig 5.2

FIGURE 5.1 (pages 90-91) and 92 (detail)

Sampling can be carried out through a small 'window' cut into the support fabric on the reverse of a tapestry, if the support fabric is degraded and likely to be replaced.
(© Historic Royal Palaces)

FIGURE 5.2 (previous page)

The Fleets Drawn up in Lines of Battle (1685).
(© Historic Royal Palaces)

FIGURE 5.3 (right)

Fireships in Action (1685).
(© Historic Royal Palaces)

FIGURE 5.4 (right, below)

Elymas the Sorcerer struck blind before Sergius Paulus (1635) (also known as *Conversion of the Proconsul*).
(The Royal Collection © 2009 Her Majesty Queen Elizabeth II)

Fig 5.3

Fig 5.4

The test case applied a scaled-down version of the MODHT project's analytical procedure and focused on answering specific questions for a conservation assessment. The tapestries were especially worthy of study, being slightly later in period to those examined for MODHT, and not as well characterised for their materials and methods as their mainland European counterparts. As conservation treatment was a priority for these tapestries, informed treatment involving scientific analysis was beneficial. Importantly, the analytical work had to be undertaken using realistic working resources and an existing budget.

The condition of each tapestry was first assessed by a textile conservator, and sampling areas were discussed and agreed between the textile conservators and scientists. Ideally, one example of each fibre type and colour from several areas of a tapestry should be taken, amounting to an average of 40 samples, but from a budgetary perspective for a routine conservation assessment and treatment project around ten samples was the affordable maximum to be submitted for analysis. The backs of the tapestries offered plenty of yarn ends which had been knotted off by the weaver, and sampling here was acceptable to both parties. For the conservator and curator, structural and pictorial yarns would remain intact so long as warps and knots were not cut, and for the scientist the MODHT research had proved that significant deterioration of yarns was also evident from the reverse side (being caused by factors besides light exposure). This major research finding warns that reverse sides of textiles are not as protected from damage as has always been presumed, despite the unfaded appearance.

Samples were carefully documented, measured, labelled, photographed and removed following the research project's protocols, as detailed below. Ten samples of wool or silk yarns of 15-20 mm each were sampled from each tapestry, representing as far as possible the basic colours of the artistic palette (red, blue, yellow, green, black, brown), because MODHT had shown that the dye and/or dyeing process for these colours had a significant effect on the condition of the dyed yarn. Where metal threads were present, up to a further five samples of silver or gold threads were also taken for simple microscopic examination. As the MODHT research had shown that silk fibres from a metal thread were not likely to be in a significantly different state of preservation compared to other silk yarns, they were not subjected to any further analysis.

Although the research did not indicate significant differences in degradation between samples taken from varying locations, it was deemed good practice to take samples from a wide region on each tapestry to minimise non-representative samples, such as large areas of re-weaving. For this reason, the combined expertise of conservator and scientist working alongside each other during sampling is invaluable. However, teamwork also helps the scientist to gain contextual information for interpretation of results, and gives the conservator an understanding of sample types best suited to answering their question. The whole process of sampling the three tapestries totalled approximately eight hours (each tapestry was already laid out and accessible for condition assessment).

Practical sampling tips

Besides the analytical expertise gained from MODHT, the practical experience was equally invaluable. Sections of tapestry were physically accessed and studied for sampling by the common conservation practice of unrolling a tapestry face-down and re-rolling it at the other end like a scroll, allowed the tapestry to be fully supported on a table at all times. This method exposed a reasonably-sized area for assessing where best to sample, while still enabling someone to reach comfortably across without resting on the tapestry and causing damage. If a tapestry had to be completely laid out for conservation treatment reasons, the sampling was best done in the process of rolling or unrolling to facilitate access to central areas in larger tapestries. The reverse side of tapestries normally have many loose ends, which MODHT demonstrated were valid for damage assessment. If the reverse side is protected with an intensively stitched support fabric that restricts access for sampling, the time and effort to remove and replace it needs to be weighed against the usefulness of analysing a small number of samples. Sometimes 'windows' can be cut into the support fabric, but

normally only where it is degraded and needs to be replaced as part of remedial conservation work before redisplay of the tapestry.

Throughout unrolling and sampling, the length of the tapestry was measured so that, with the width distance (measured from the bottom edge), the sample sites could be expressed as a co-ordinate. It was critical that removal of the yarn did not weaken the woven structure by cutting a warp, or affect the image by removing a weft knot. Before snipping off the sample its exact site was photographed, showing the yarn resting on a small white label with its sample reference number. When necessary, a small cocktail stick was ideal for pinpointing an exact yarn. Besides documentation, photographs proved useful for interpreting scientific results. For example, when trace red dye components were detected for a yellow yarn but the

FIGURE 5.5

Accessing threads on the back of a tapestry for sampling, fortunately exposed by the support fabric.
(© Historic Royal Palaces)

photograph showed no red threads in the immediate sampling area, this suggested an intentional dye combination.

The minimum yarn length, calculated as 5 mm per analytical test to be undertaken, was removed with sharp needlework scissors and fine-point tweezers and placed immediately in an inert sample vial labelled with the exact reference number in the photograph [Figs 5.5, 6]. This reference number had to be unique to enable a researcher to identify from which tapestry the sample was taken (by association with the textile's official accession number, given by the collection's institution) and the precise area from which it was taken (by cross-referencing with the sampling record). The reference number developed for use in the MODHT project was two-part: the alphabetic part of the code represented the collection the piece belonged to, and an accompanying correlative number indicated the particular piece within each collection and was the code for the samples to be analysed (for example BRU1/1, BRU1/2,

and so on). The code BRU stood for the tapestries belonging to the two Bruges' Museums, the Musées Communaux and the Musée Notre-Dame de la Poterie. BXL was the code for the collection of the Royal Museum of Art and History of Brussels. HRP was for the Hampton Court Palace collection, PNM for the collection of Patrimonio Nacional at the Palacio Real in Madrid, and finally TOU for the collection of Tournai Cathedral.

The required sample size was slightly less than that for the MODHT research because the experimental procedure improved. All historical samples are a valuable and finite resource, so any sample material remaining after analysis needs to be archived carefully. The recording of a sample completely destroyed during analysis eliminates any confusion that a sample has gone astray. The complete documentation procedure (measure-

FIGURE 5.6

Pinpointing the exact sample taken for analysis.
(© Historic Royal Palaces)

ment, photographs, vial labelling, analysis, reporting and archiving) should be consistent in the sample's reference number. An open-ended, adaptable reference method is most useful for continuity into future work.

Analysis – methods used, results and comparison to MODHT

Questions asked for the case study were: what materials had been used, how do English and Flemish tapestries compare in their construction materials, and how strong relatively were the three tapestries? Answering them necessitated three analytical approaches derived from MODHT. First was dye analysis by PDA-HPLC because different dyes affected the strength of wool and silk tapestry yarns, and their sources informed provenance and trade, dating and past restoration knowledge for art historical evidence. Second, amino acid analysis by HPLC would provide a clear marker of chemical damage for both wool and silk from their proteins. Third and finally, for silk yarns only, size exclusion chromatography (SEC) would measure a marker indicative of tensile strength. Full details for each technique are given in chapter 3 and appendix 1. All three methods destroy the sample, leaving just one chance per test for a result.

Dye analysis

The colour palette for all three tapestries in this case study was achieved with natural dyes: madder, redwood and cochineal for red; weld and other luteolin-based sources for yellow and green; woad or indigo sources for blue; and tannins for brown. Most colours were a combination of between two and four dyes. All the dyes were typical for textiles of the period and also identified in the MODHT tapestries, which were made earlier. Synthetic dyestuffs were not detected, suggesting no re-weaving in the sampled areas since the mid-19th century.

Amino acid degradation of wool and silk from the English tapestries followed the trends of the 16th-century Flemish tapestries studied during the MODHT project. In fact, the general level of degradation for all the tapestries from Hampton Court Palace analysed between the test case study and full MODHT research project was very similar. Within the test case group, silk from the slightly earlier *Elymas the Sorcerer struck blind before Sergius Paulus* tapestry was relatively more degraded than the two 'Battle of the Solebay' tapestries, in agreement with visual observations from conservators' condition assessments. Although few samples were taken for the test case (especially of silk, which reduced the opportunities to compare data between scientific techniques), silk analysed by both amino acid analysis and SEC showed good agreement for degradation trends [see Figure 5.8, page 100].

Between the two 'Battle of the Solebay' tapestries, *The Fleets Drawn up in Lines of Battle* was in a slightly better state than the other, measuring slightly higher average percentages for tyrosine (silk) and cysteic acid (wool).

While there was no apparent correlation between fibre strength and a single dye, perhaps because most were combinations and multiple sources could most likely mask the effects of an individual dye, yarns coloured with three and four dyes tended to measure the higher levels of degradation. Conversely, the samples dyed with only one or two dye components (e.g. only tannin, or

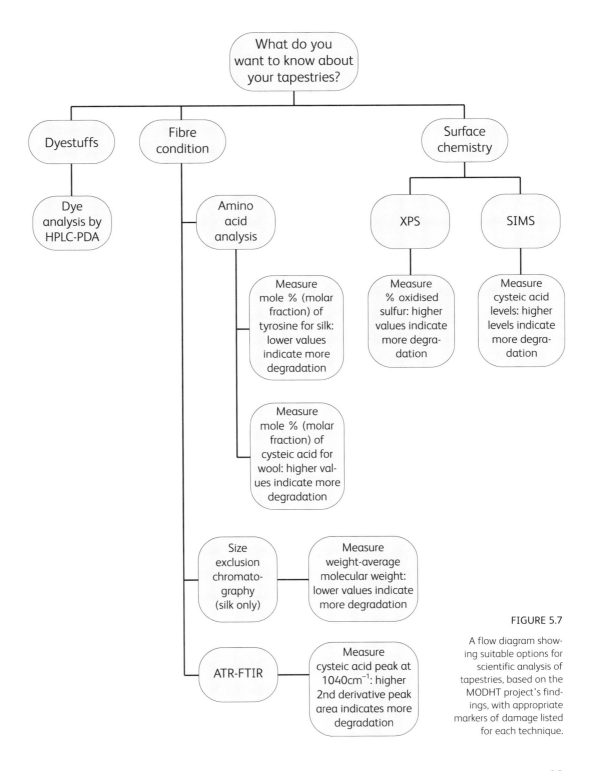

FIGURE 5.7

A flow diagram showing suitable options for scientific analysis of tapestries, based on the MODHT project's findings, with appropriate markers of damage listed for each technique.

madder and tannin) were in a comparatively better state of preservation. This trend was particularly evident in the wool samples.

Conclusions

Amino acid analysis enabled the three tapestries to be ranked in order of relative chemical degradation of the fibres. As a complementary technique, SEC analysis was useful, although its restricted application to silk is a drawback, especially when silk tapestry yarns are more likely to be restored because they degrade faster than wool. Indeed, the two 'Solebay' tapestries were thought to contain much re-woven silk. Although great care was taken to identify 'original' yarns, silk samples with a high molecular weight or % tyrosine might feasibly have been restoration threads rather than particularly well-preserved originals. The dyes did not appear to contribute to fibre strength as clearly as they did for MODHT,

although the more times a wool yarn was over-dyed, the weaker it became, as might be expected.

The similarity in conclusions between the test case study and the research project are encouraging, yet almost expected because the case study results were interpreted on the findings of a unique research project. Nonetheless, the exercise has demonstrated the viability of gaining useful scientific information from a reduced sample set (approximately one quarter scale). As always, analysing small numbers of samples introduces risks that the set is not representative of the whole textile and/or misses outliers beyond the 'norm', such as rarer yarns or dyestuffs which prove more interesting or diagnostic. Integrating scientific analysis into routine conservation treatment programmes entails striking a reasonable balance between maximising the amount of information while minimising

FIGURE 5.8

Graph illustrating good correlation between amino acid analysis and SEC for test case study silk samples.

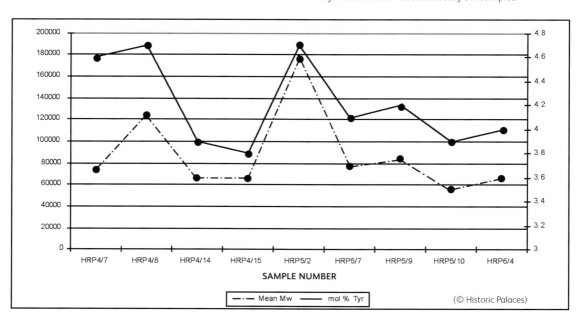

(© Historic Palaces)

staff time, analysis costs and sample destruction.

This case study exercise has shown that a greatly reduced number of samples, coupled with only one or two of the more common scientific techniques, can still provide valid and useful information about the level of degradation in a tapestry. Using the sampling protocols described in this chapter, a limited number of yarns can be sampled as part of the routine conservation treatment of a tapestry: for example, during a condition assessment, photography or when testing for wet-fastness. The samples can be analysed using well-established techniques (such as amino acid analysis or FTIR) which are available on a commercial basis, at most universities, and in the laboratories of some national museums and galleries. While analysis adds a cost to the conservation project, it is a small fraction (typically between 1-10 per cent) of the total cost of a full tapestry conservation treatment. The measurement of chemical markers of damage, as described in this chapter, provides evidence which can be used to prioritise more efficiently the treatment of one tapestry over another; and indeed to rationalize the large cost of interventive treatment itself.

Three of the most useful assessment techniques are all HPLC-based, but because they need the compounds of interest to be in solution, the sample is destroyed and unavailable for further testing. Non-destructive methods that indicate a reliable level of relevant information are therefore valuable for screening prior to sample-destructive analysis. For example, although the level of information from ATR-FTIR, SIMS and 3D Fluorescence is sometimes secondary to the more informative chromatographic methods, they are nonetheless useful because they can indicate whether a fibre protein is present or altered, or a fibre is dyed with an organic colourant.

It therefore makes sense to apply non-

FIGURE 5.9 – Table of sample sizes required for analysis			
Analysis	**Technique**	**Minimum yarn length**	**Is the sample destroyed?**
Dyes	HPLC-PDA	5 mm	Yes
Amino acids	HPLC	5 mm	Yes
Fibre chain lengths	HPLC	5 mm	Yes
Amino acids	ATR-FTIR	5 mm	No
Amino acids	XPS	2 mm	Yes
Amino acids	SIMS	2 mm	No
Screening for dyes	3D Fluorescence	5 mm	No

destructive techniques, for instance ATR-FTIR (and SIMS if available), at the beginning of the analytical project so that the sample can be recovered and reanalysed using another method or one that is destructive. If more than one HPLC analysis is necessary, e.g. dyes and amino acids, the sample must be big enough to divide into multiple minimum lengths (in this example, at least 10 mm long), because each will need to be chemically prepared in a specific way for each type of analysis and is normally destroyed in the process.

The legacy of the MODHT project: work by other research groups

As with most research projects, the MODHT research has highlighted many more questions than could be answered immediately. Other researchers have also been at work in this area, to inform and widen the study of tapestry conservation. It is important to acknowledge that MODHT is not the only research project considering the problems of conserving historic tapestries. Of particular note is a complementary research project 'In-situ Monitoring of Tapestry Degradation using Strain-based Engineering Techniques' at the University of Southampton, which brought together researchers within the School of Engineering Sciences and the Textile Conservation Centre (TCC) in a three-year study (2007-2009). The project, funded by the Arts and Humanities Research Council (AHRC), employed a post-doctoral researcher and two PhD students, and benefited from the involvement of partners within the fields of conservation and engineering. The research included tests on both modern tapestries, specially woven at the West Dean Tapestry Weaving Studio, and historic tapestries. The research was supported by partners in the conservation field: Historic Royal Palaces, the National Trust and English Heritage. It followed on from a pilot study by the same team beginning in 2003, which reported to a group of tapestry conservators and scientists in 2005.

Whereas MODHT concentrated on chemical methods of analysis, this project looked at the effect of mechanical strain on tapestries hanging on display, and how this may be monitored and quantified. Frances Lennard of the TCC commented:

> It is often the case that parallel strands of research develop at the same time. It is exciting when such projects interrelate in the way that the MODHT and University of Southampton projects have done, investigating different aspects of a common problem. One tangible legacy of the MODHT research is Kathryn Hallett's involvement on the Advisory Panel of the University of Southampton project. The net result of these complementary projects will be to enhance the long-term future of historic tapestries.

The University of Southampton research explored the physio-mechanical properties of these large and heavy textiles on display – the forces experienced in a hanging tapestry and how best to monitor and ameliorate any negative effects. The project aimed to establish a non-destructive testing methodology for measuring strain and monitoring damage in tapestries hanging under their own weight and when supported by backing fabrics. The research focuses on how to quantify the rate of degradation for a given hanging configuration and how to determine the variables that affect the rate of degradation. The experimental work applied a whole-field non-destructive technique to identify damaged regions, used in conjunction with strain measurements taken from optical fibre sensors. The focus of the work was the successful integration of the two techniques. A long term aim of the project was to apply this methodology to investigate different methods of treating tapestries. Outcomes of the two University of Southampton projects include the following:

Dulieu-Barton, J. M., Dokos, L., Eastop, D. E., Lennard, F. J., Chambers, A. R. and M. Sahin (2005): 'Deformation and strain measurement techniques for the inspection of damage in works of art', in *Reviews in Conservation*, vol. 6, pp. 61-71.

Dulieu-Barton, J. M., Sahin, M., Lennard, F. J., Eastop, D. E. and A. R. Chambers (2007): 'Assessing the feasibility of monitoring the condition of historic tapestries using engineering techniques', in *Key Engineering Materials*, vol. 347, pp. 187-92.

Lennard, F. J., Eastop, D. E., Dulieu-Barton, J. M., Ye, C. C., Khennouf, D., Chambers, A. R. and H. Williams (2008): 'Progress in strain monitoring of tapestries', *Postprints of ICOM Committee for Conservation*, 15th Triennial meeting, New Delhi, India, 22-26 September 2008.

Sahin, M., Chambers, A. R., Dokos, L., Dulieu-Barton, J. M., Earl, J., Eastop, D. E. and Lennard, F. J. (2006): 'Mechanical testing and its role in the condition assessment of tapestries', in F. J. Lennard and M. Hayward (eds): *Tapestry Conservation: Principles and Practice* (Oxford: Elsevier), pp. 227-34.

While focusing attention on recent and current research, it is important not to overlook some of the pioneering, though more restricted, studies undertaken in the heritage conservation sector in the 1990s. These include work by Ballard (1996), Howell (1996, 1997), and by Boersma and Hoffenk de Graaf (1996, 1997). It is also important to note a recent study on the fore-topsail of HMS *Victory* (Garside, 2005) in which physico-chemical analysis informed decisions about whether it was safe to hang the huge sail for display.

Ballard, M. W. (1996): 'Hanging out: strength, elongation, and relative humidity: some physical properties of textile fibers', in J. Bridgland (ed.) *Preprints of ICOM Committee for Conservation*, 11th Triennial meeting, Edinburgh, 1-6 September 1996 (London: James & James), pp. 665-69.

Bilson, T., Cooke, B. and D. Howell (1997): 'Mechanical aspects of lining "loose hung" textiles', in *Fabric of an exhibition: An interdisciplinary approach – Preprints* (Ottawa: Canadian Conservation Institute), pp. 63-69.

Garside, P. and P. Wyeth (2005): 'Assessing the physical state of the fore-topsail of the HMS Victory', in R. Janaway and P. Wyeth (eds): *Scientific Analysis of Ancient and Historic Textiles: Informing Preservation, Display and Interpretation* (London: Archetype), pp. 118-25.

Hofenk de Graaff, J. and F. Boersma (1996): *Tapestry Conservation. Support Methods and Fabrics for Tapestries. Results of the Questionnaire on the Subject of Tapestry Conservation* (Netherlands Institute for Cultural Heritage).

Hofenk de Graaff, J. and F. Boersma (1997): *Tapestry Conservation. Support Methods and Fabrics for Tapestries. Part I Tapestries. General Background Information. Part II Chemistry and Physics of Flax (Linen) and Cotton* (Netherlands Institute for Cultural Heritage).

Howell, D. (1996): 'Some mechanical effects of inappropriate humidity on textiles', in J. Bridgland (ed.): *Preprints of ICOM Committee for Conservation*, 11th Triennial meeting, Edinburgh, 1-6 September 1996 (London: James & James), pp. 692-98.

Looking forward

MODHT adds to the ever-growing number of collaborative partnerships between conservator, curator and scientist for the preservation of historical collections. Other examples, among many, funded by the European Community include:

- 'Improved Damage Assessment of Parchment, IDAP', a research project concerned with the preservation of parchment materials (further information is available at: www.idap-parchment.dk).
- 'Innovative Modelling of Museum Pollution and Conservation Thresholds, IMPACT', which produced a web-based software tool to assist museums, galleries and archives in assessing risks posed to their collections by air pollution (further information is available at: www.ucl.ac.uk/sustainableheritage/impact).
- 'A Light Dosimeter for Monitoring Cultural Heritage: Development, Testing and Transfer to Market, LiDo', which developed sensitive light dosimeters for monitoring cultural heritage (further information is available at www.lido.fhg.de – and www.lightcheck.co.uk).
- 'Preventive Conservation Strategies for Protection of Organic Objects in Museums, Historic Buildings and Archives, MASTER', a project which developed an early warning system based on an effect sensor for organic materials (further information is available at: www.nilu.no/master).
- 'Microclimate Indoor Monitoring in Cultural Heritage Preservation, MIMIC', which developed paint damage dosimeters and a new dosimeter using piezoelectric quartz crystal technology to monitor pollutants (further information is available at: http://iaq.dk/mimic).

The beneficial leap forward in information from the MODHT research opens the door further to achieving meaningful results with fewer samples in real-life situations. The results and conclusions drawn so far demand that more research and case studies are undertaken on tapestries to strengthen and improve the routine use of chemical markers for their damage assessment. With the project having successfully shown how scientific analysis can support and complement conservation and curatorial decisions for tapestry preservation, and that highly-resourced research is translatable into realistic working practices, it would be encouraging to see the outcomes fertilised with new ideas and to develop with increasing application. If MODHT inspires or encourages others, as it has the project team, it will have served a worthy purpose.

FIGURE 5.10

Tapestry conservation detail.
(The Royal Collection
© 2009 Her Majesty Queen Elizabeth II)

Technical Details and Protocols for Scientific Analysis

Marei Hacke, Kathryn Hallett, Marianne Odlyha, David Peggie, Anita Quye and Ina Vanden Berghe

Dye analysis by PDA HPLC and LC-MS

Natural dyes are complex mixtures of organic chemicals. Some dyes contain compounds with wide-ranging properties, while others have compounds that are very similar to each other. Not only that, but colours like green, orange, brown, black and purple were often traditionally made by mixing different dyes. None of this is known until the dye is analysed, and with historical textiles like the MODHT tapestries there is normally only enough sample for one analysis.

The best analytical method for natural dyes on historical textiles is high performance liquid chromatography with photodiode array detection (PDA HPLC).[1-3] The chromatographic system involves pumping a water-based mobile phase modified with methanol or acetonitrile through a stationary phase of non-polar modified silica or a polymeric hybrid material held inside a column. When a sample is injected into the mobile phase, it is carried through the stationary phase and the sample's chemical components (called analytes) are separated by a partitioning mechanism between the two phases. With the correct mobile phase composition and elution conditions, it is possible to separate out the important analytes that characterise many species of dyeing plants, lichens and scale insects. A HPLC system with a pump that changes the solvent modifier propor-

tions in the mobile phase during analysis is the most versatile for natural dyes.

The photo diode array (PDA) detector relies on the dye analytes being able to absorb ultraviolet (UV) and/or visible light. After chromatographic separation, the analytes pass through a detector containing photo diode cells. Each photo diode is sensitive over a small and discrete wavelength, but collectively they cover a wide spectrum in the UV-Visible range, typically from 250 nm to 750 nm. With software manipulation, all the spectral information for each analyte is rapidly combined, resulting in a UV-Visible spectrum. By comparing each unknown analyte's spectrum and the time taken from injection of the sample into the HPLC system until detection (called retention time) with libraries for known compounds, a chemical profile for the dye is built up which enables it to be identified.

Samples for PDA HPLC analysis need to be in a liquid form. For MODHT samples this involved chemically stripping the dye off the yarn. To do this, between 0.1 mg and 5 mg of sample was placed in a 2 ml tapered glass test tube and 400 µl of a 2:1:1 (v/v/v) mixture of 37% hydrochloric acid: methanol: water added. The tube was then heated in a water bath at 100°C for precisely 10 minutes. After rapidly cooling the outside of the test tube carefully under cold running water, the extract was filtered using a 5 µm polypropylene frit (Analytichem) under positive pressure. The test tube was then rinsed with 200 μl methanol and the combined filtrates dried by rotary vacuum evaporation over a water bath at 40°C. When the extract was ready to be analysed, its dry residue was reconstituted with 25 μl methanol and 25 μl water. If analysis was not possible within 6 hours, the dried sample was stored in a freezer at -18°C.

The HPLC stationary phase used for MODHT was a Phenomenex Sphereclone™ ODS2 (5 μm particle size) packed in a column measuring 150 mm × 4.6 mm (length × internal diameter) and fitted with a guard column containing the same stationary phase. The column was enclosed in a heat-controlled chamber maintained at 25±1°C. 20 μl of the sample extract was injected via a Rheodyne injector with a 25 μl sample loop. The mobile phase conditions were controlled by a gradient pump (Waters™ 600), following a programme for three solvents: (A) 20% methanol (aq); (B) 100% methanol; and (C) 5% v/v phosphoric acid (aq). The gradient programme started isocratically at 67%A: 23%B: 10%C and was held for 3 minutes. It then ramped to 0%A: 90%B: 10%C as a linear gradient from 3 to 29 minutes. From 29 to 30 minutes, a linear gradient changed the proportions back to 67%A: 23%B: 10%C. This was held isocratically from 30 to 35 minutes to equilibrate the chromatographic system before injecting the next sample. All solvents for the mobile phase were chromatography-grade (Romil and Merck-BDH) and the water was deionised. The mobile phase was sparged using a vacuum in-line degasser. The PDA detector (Waters™ 2996) measured spectral information between 250 nm and 750 nm at a bandwidth (resolution) of 2.4 nm and response time of 1 s, with the chromatographed peaks monitored at 254 nm. The pump and detector were controlled by Waters' 'Empower'™ software which also collected and manipulated the data. The total run time was 35 minutes at a mobile phase flow rate of 1.2 ml min[-1]. An example of the results is shown in Fig. A.1 (see p. 108).

Mass spectrometry (MS) coupled with HPLC (LC-MS) is a powerful method for characterising unknown organic components.[4-9] The analytes exit from HPLC and enter the MS where they are bombarded with ionised particles. A 'fingerprint' of the charged particles is then formed from the analytes' mass to charge (m/z) ratios. The additional use of an ion trap device with the MS (called MS[n]) enables analytes to be repeatedly broken down so that their chemical structure can be pieced together from highly characteristic patterns.[7] Applying LC-MS and LC-MS[n] to MODHT resulted in cochineal being analysed in the greatest detail so far,[8] and identification of sawwort's light-ageing degradation compounds.[9]

The system used was a Finnigan Mat Spectra™ system (an AS3000 autosampler, a P4000 pump and V2000 single wavelength, tuneable UV-visible detector). It was connected to a Thermoquest Finnigan LCQ™ mass spectrometer operating in negative ion mode and controlled by LCQ Navigator™ software. The autosampler delivered 20 μL of sample (in methanol) into a chromatographic system with the same column and gradient system as the HPLC PDA analysis, although a post-column splitter reduced the flow into the mass spectrometer to approximately 0.30 mL min. For MS[n] experiments, the relative collision energy was usually around 20-25%. All data was collected and processed by the LCQ Navigator™ software.

References

1. Quye, A., Cheape, H., Burnett, J., Ferreira, E. S. B, Hulme, A. N. and H. McNab (2003): 'An historical and analytical study of red, pink, green and yellow colours in quality 18th- and early 19th-century Scottish tartans', in *Dyes in History and Archaeology*, vol. 19, pp. 1-12.
2. Petroviciu, I. and J. Wouters (2002): 'Analysis of natural dyes from Romanian 19th- and 20th-

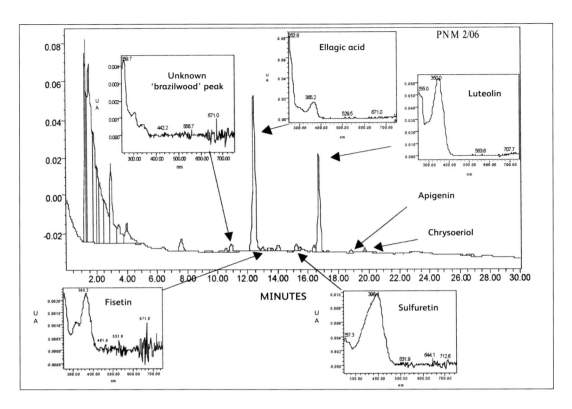

FIGURE A.1

The PDA HPLC chromatogram (monitored at 254nm) of the acid hydrolysed extract from sample PNM 2/06, a yellow silk yarn. Characteristic components for young fustic (ellagic acid, fisetin and sulfuretin), weld (luteolin, apigenin and chrysoeriol) and brazilwood (a distinctive and consistent marker, although still unknown) were identified. (© National Museums Scotland)

century ethnographical textiles by DAD-HPLC', in *Dyes in History and Archaeology*, vol. 18, pp. 57-69.

3. Trojanowicz, M., Orska-Gawryś, J., Surowiec, I., Szostek, B., Urbaniak-Walczak, K., Kehl, J. and M. Wrobel (2004): 'Chromatographic investigation of dyes extracted from coptic textiles from the national museum in Warsaw', in *Studies in Conservation*, vol. 49, pp. 115-30.

4. Puchalska, M., Poleć-Pawlak, K., Zadrozna, I., Hryszko, H. and M. Jarosz (2004): 'Identification of indigoid dyes in natural organic pigments used in historical art objects by high-performance liquid chromatography coupled to electrospray ionisation mass spectrometry', in *Journal of Mass Spectrometry*, vol. 39, pp. 1441-49.

5. Ferreira, E. S. B. (2002): 'New approaches towards the identification of yellow dyes in ancient textiles', PhD Thesis (University of Edinburgh).

6. Peggie, D. A. (2006): 'The development and application of analytical methods for the identification of dyes on historical textiles', PhD Thesis (University of Edinburgh).

7. Ferreira, E. S. B., Quye, A., Hulme, A. N. and H. McNab (2003): 'LC-Ion Trap MS and PDA-HPLC – Complementary techniques in the analysis of flavonoid dyes in historical textiles: The case study of an 18th century herald's tabard', in *Dyes in History and Archaeology*, vol. 19, pp. 13-18.

8. Peggie, D. A., Hulme, A. N., McNab, H. and A. Quye (2008): 'Towards the identification of characteristic minor components from textiles dyed with weld (*Reseda luteola* L.) and those dyed with Mexican cochineal (*Dactylopius coccus* Costa)', in *Microchima Acta*, vol. 162, pp. 371-80.

9. Hulme, A. N., McNab, H., Peggie, D. A. and A. Quye (accepted): 'The chemical characterisation of aged and unaged fibre samples dyed with sawwort (*Serratula Tinctoria*) using PDA HPLC and HPLC ESI MS', in *Dyes in History and Archaeology*, vol. 22.

Amino acid analysis by HPLC

Keratin and fibroin, the main structural proteins of wool and silk respectively, are composed of multiple amino acids; wool has 18 amino acids and silk has 16.[1,2] The relative amounts of amino acids can be used for identifying wool and silk, and changes to the amino acid composition used as indicators of degradation.[3-6] Analysis by high performance liquid chromatography with fluorescence detection (HPLC-fluo) was used for MODHT because it is a highly sensitive technique requiring very small sample sizes. Just 1μg of protein sample was ample to reveal its amino acid composition.

Each yarn sample was first broken down into single α-amino acids by acid hydrolysis in oxygen-free conditions using 6 N HCl and 1% phenol in the gas phase. A fluorescent reagent was then added using a pre-derivatisation system (Waters AccQ-Fluor reagent kit).[7] The solution of amino acid derivatives was separated by HPLC as described for dye analysis (see above) using a temperature-controlled stationary phase (C18 column) and a gradient elution mobile phase. A scanning fluorescence detector measured the fluorescence emission of each separated amino acid derivative at 395 nm with excitation at 250 nm. A full description of the procedure can be found in other publications.[5, 6]

The amount of each α-amino acid detected was calculated by calibration with a commercially available standard solution containing well defined amounts of each of the following amino acids: aspartic and glutamic acids, serine, glycine, histidine, arginine, threonine, alanine, proline, tyrosine, valine, methionine, lysine, isoleucine, leucine, phenylanaline and cystine.

Development of HPLC-fluo for MODHT led to a sensitive and practical identification method for wool degradation marker. The amino acid cystine that is present in wool's keratin protein exists naturally in equilibrium

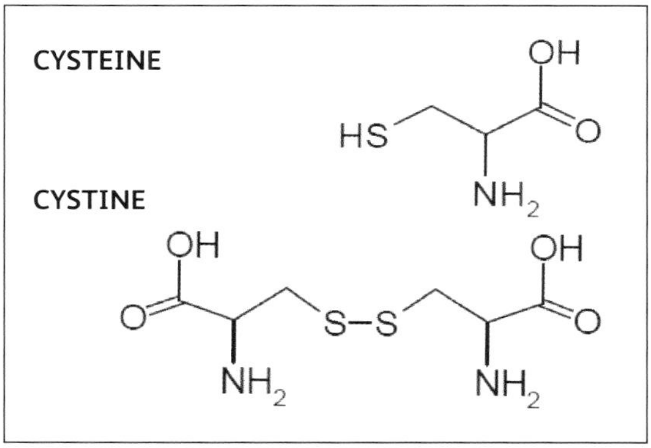

FIGURE A.2

Chemical structure of the amino acids cystine and cysteine.
(© Royal Institute for Cultural Heritage, Belgium)

with its reduced form, cysteine. Both amino acids are unstable and therefore difficult to quantify by analysis. Treating a wool sample with performic acid before the acid hydrolysis step in the analysis would oxidise both amino acids to the more stable cysteic acid, thereby enabling the total amount to be quantified. This was successfully tested on 20 selected historic wool samples, but unexpectedly and fortuitously it was found that cysteic acid was already present in detectable amounts in the untreated samples. This demonstrated that cystine and cysteine were being oxidised to cysteic acid in naturally-aged wool and at detectable levels.

Cysteic acid was therefore found to be a highly useful marker for aged wool oxidation, with the analytical method requiring only the simple addition of a cysteic acid mono-standard to make it applicable for MODHT. By combining cysteic acid with the analytical information for all the other oxidisable amino acids, a specific wool degradation parameter could be measured. This was the 'keratin oxidation factor (KOF)', calculated from the ratio of the molar fractions of lysine, histidine, tyrosine and methionine to those for aspartic, glutamic and cysteic acid (arginine was not taken into account).

References

1. Asquith R. S. (1977): *Chemistry of Natural Protein Fibers* (New York: Plenum Press), pp. 56-58.
2. Asquith (1977): ibid.
3. Schilling M. R. and H. P. Khanjian (1996): 'Gas chromatographic analysis of amino acids as ethyl chloroformate derivates. III. Identification of proteinaceous binding media by interpretation of amino acid composition data', in *ICOM Committee for Conservation*, 11th Triennial Meeting (Preprints) (Edinburgh), pp. 211-19.
4. Wouters J., Van Bos, M. and K. Lamens (2000): 'Baroque stucco marble decorations I. Preparation of laboratory replicas and establishment of criteria for analytical evaluation of organic materials', in *Studies in Conservation*, vol. 45, pp. 106-16.
5. Wouters J., Van Bos, M. and K. Lamens (2000): 'Baroque stucco marble decorations II. Composition and degradation of the organic materials in historical samples and implications for their conservation', in *Studies in Conservation*, vol. 45, pp. 169-79.
6. Vanden Berghe, I. and J. Wouters (2005): 'Identification and condition evaluation of deteriorated protein fibres at the sub-microgram level by calibrated amino acid analysis', in *Scientific Analysis of Ancient and Historic Textiles: Informing Preservation, Display and Interpretation*, AHRB Research Centre for Textile Conservation and Textile Studies First Annual Conference, 13-15 July 2004 (Textile Conservation Centre, Winchester Campus, University of Southampton, UK), pp. 151-58.
7. Waters AccQ.Tag Chemistry Package Instruction Manual (1993), (Millipore Corporation, Milford): Manual number WAT052874.

Fibre degradation by size exclusion chromatography

Size exclusion chromatography (SEC) is a well-established technique for the production of molecular weight distributions in polymers.[1-9] It is a type of high performance liquid chromatography (HPLC) which separates sample molecules according to the hydrodynamic volume of the polymer molecules (the hydrodynamic volume is the space a polymer molecule takes up when in solution).

The approximate molecular weight can then be deduced because the exact relationship between molecular weight and hydrodynamic volume is calibrated using standards of known molecular weight. However, the relationship between molecular weight and hydrodynamic volume depends on several variables, so this is not an absolute measurement technique.

1.5 mg of each sample was dissolved in 0.4 ml concentrated lithium thiocyanate (LiSCN) solution. Gentle agitation was used to complete the dissolution. Samples were filtered to 0.45 μm using centrifuge microfiltration. 20 μl silk solution was injected to the SEC system (PerkinElmer Series 200 HLPC), using a flow rate of 0.3 ml/min, total run time of 30 minutes per sample. The mobile phase was 8M urea, which denatures (uncoils) the protein in solution, run at a constant temperature of 30°C. The column used was a Phenomenex BIOSEP™ S-4000 with guard column. The column was calibrated using narrow standard calibration markers with detection of UV absorbance at 280 nm, meaning the results should be considered as relative, rather than absolute molecular weights. After running the series of narrow standards, a polynomial fit was then performed (third order), and the resulting log M vs. retention time (or volume) calibration curve was plotted.

Since SEC produces a molecular weight distribution, it is important to utilise this when expressing data. For example, quoting the single figure modal average, such as the Mp (molecular weight of the peak), will provide no information about the breadth or intensity of that peak. There are two averaged values that can be calculated to take account of the peak distribution. The number-average molecular weight (Mn) is the total weight of all the polymer molecules in a sample, divided by the total number of polymer molecules in a sample. The weight-average molecular weight, Mw, can also be calculated: it is biased towards the heavier molecules. The weight average is based on the fact that a bigger molecule contains more of the total mass of the polymer sample than the smaller molecules. Mn and Mw can be correlated to various types of polymer properties. The tensile strength is often most influenced by the large molecules in the material (related to the Mw). For this reason, the Mw value has been used for most of the data analysis during the MODHT project.

One of the difficulties with the existing method prior to the MODHT project was that the LiSCN solvent was also detected at the optimum detection wavelength for silk (280 nm). This resulted in chromatograms with two partially resolved peaks – one for the silk sample and one for the LiSCN solvent [Figs A.3 and A.4]. One of the many method improvements carried out during the MODHT project was to separate or resolve these two peaks by denaturing the silk during the analysis. Denaturation involved adding 8M urea to the mobile phase to disrupt the

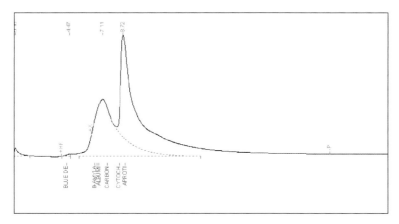

FIGURE A.3

Co-elution of silk and LiSCN solvent peak using original SEC method.
(© Historic Palaces)

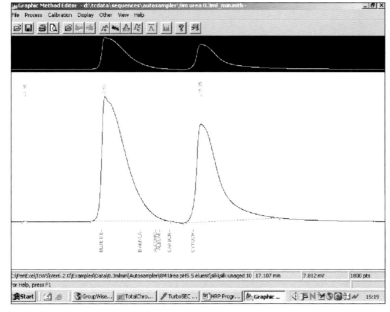

FIGURE A.4

Separation of silk and LiSCN peaks using the method improved during MODHT.
(© Historic Palaces)

intramolecular bonds holding together the tertiary structure of the protein. When denatured, proteins transform from their native globular structure to a 'rod-like' unfolded conformation. The length of the polymer chains is unaffected, so that the SEC method can still be applied. However, when unfolded, the denatured molecules take up a larger space, so the hydrodynamic volume is altered. The molecules therefore pass through the column more rapidly, because they are less able to penetrate the pores than in the native state. The LiSCN was unaffected by the denaturing conditions, so continued to elute at the original time. Thus, the silk and solvent peaks were resolved [Fig. A.4]. The calibration standards were also run in denaturing conditions to allow for this change.

References

1. Bos, J. (2002): 'Size exclusion chromatography as a tool in the investigation of archaeological objects', in *Contributions to Conservation: Research in Conservation at the Netherlands Institute for Cultural Heritage* (ICN) (J. Mosk and N. Tennent, eds) (James & James [Science Publishers] Ltd: London), pp. 10-15.
2. Burgess, H. (1982): 'The use of gel permeation chromatography in investigating the degradation of cellulose during conservation bleaching', in *Science and Technology in the Service of Conservation. Preprints of the Contributions to the Washington Congress, 3-9 September 1982* (N. Brommelle and G. Thomson, eds) (International Institute for Conservation: London), pp. 85-88.
3. Dupont, A.-L. (2002): 'The role of gelatine/alum sizing in the degradation of paper: a study by size exclusion chromatography in lithium chloride/ N,N-dimethylacetamide using multiangle light scattering detection', in *Works of Art on Paper, Books, Documents and Photographs: Techniques and Conservation. Contributions to the Baltimore Congress, 2-6 September 2002* (V. Daniels, A. Donnithorne and P. Smith, eds) (International Institute for Conservation: London), pp. 59-64.
4. Emsley, A., Ali, M. and R. Heywood (2000): 'A size exclusion chromatography study of cellulose degradation', in *Polymer*, vol. 41, pp. 8513-21.
5. Jerosch, H., Lavédrine, B. and J.-C. Cherton (2002): 'Study on the correlation between SEC and mechanical tests of different paper types for degradation state evaluation', in *Restaurator*, vol. 23, pp. 222-39.
6. Pryde, A. and M. Gilbert (1980): *Applications of High Performance Liquid Chromatography* (Chapman and Hall: London).
7. Trathnigg, B. (2000): 'Size-exclusion chromatography of polymers', in *Encyclopedia of Analytical Chemistry* (R. A. Meyers, ed.) (John Wiley & Sons Ltd, Chichester), pp. 8008-34.
8. Tse, S. and Dupont, A.-L. (1998): 'Measuring silk deterioration: investigation into the usefulness of high performance size exclusion chromatography, viscosity and electrophoresis', in *Abstracts of Papers of the American Chemical Society*, vol. 216, p. 43.
9. Tse, S. and Dupont, A.-L. (2001): 'Measuring silk deterioration by high performance size-exclusion chromatography, viscometry and electrophoresis', in *Historic Textiles, Papers, and Polymers in Museums* (ACS Symposium Series 779) (J. Cardamone and M. Baker, eds) (American Chemical Society: Washington DC), pp. 98-114.

Wool degradation by Fourier Transform Infrared (FTIR) spectroscopy

Infrared (IR) spectroscopy belongs to the group of analytical techniques based on molecular vibrations within materials.[1,2] IR spectroscopy requires the irradiation of a sample with light in the mid-IR part of the electromagnetic spectrum (4000 to 400 cm^{-1}). The light transmitted, through or absorbed by, the substance is measured using a sensitive detector system. Absorption occurs if the wavelength of the incident IR radiation coincides with the frequency of oscillation of a molecular bond and leads to simple stretching, bending and twisting motions of functional groups. Since each of these vibrational modes is present as different absorbance peaks in an infrared spectrum, IR spectroscopy can assist with structural identification.

Wool degradation for MODHT was

FIG. A.5 – Characteristic infrared spectral frequencies for wool

Species	Structure	Wave-number (cm^{-1})
CO stretching, Amide I	–C=O	1650
NH deformation, Amide II	–NH	1540
NH and OCN mixed vibration, Amide III	–N–H &	1230
Cystine dioxide	–N–CO	1121
Cystine monoxide	–SO$_2$–S–	1071
Cysteic acid	–SO$_2^-$	1040
S-sulphonate (Bunte salt)	–S–SO$_3^-$	1022

studied by Attenuated Total Reflectance-Fourier Transform Infrared (ATR-FTIR) using a Perkin-Elmer 2000 FTIR spectrometer equipped with a TGS detector and a 'SensIR Technologies' Durascope™ placed in the sample compartment with a diamond internal reflectance element (IRE) at 45° to the incident beam. Using these conditions the depth of penetration into the sample at 1050 cm^{-1} was approximately 2 µm.[3]

Spectra were recorded with the exposed side of the thread or fabric against the IRE, using the Durascope to regulate the contact force between sample and the diamond crystal so that measurements were reproducible. Data were processed using GRAMS32 AI software (Galactic®) at 16 scans per spectrum, with all spectra normalised at the peak height of Amide III (1232 cm^{-1}).[4] Using the characteristic spectral bands for proteins in wool shown in Fig. A.5 (above), the area of the relevant signal (in this case, cysteic acid) in the second-derivative spectrum was then measured and used as the marker of damage.

Light-aged wool samples showed changes in the Amide I and Amide II spectral regions. The reduced height of the Amide I band was attributed to the breaking of peptide bonds, with peak broadening around 1670 cm^{-1} indicating an increasingly disordered structure. Spectral changes in the region of 1720 cm^{-1} were possibly the formation of fatty acids from oxidised lipids in wool because fatty acids contain a carbonyl group that absorbs infrared radiation between 1715 and 1725 cm^{-1}.[5] High levels of light exposure (30 Mlux.hrs) resulted in a decrease in the intensity of the Amide II band (1538 cm^{-1}) along with broadening of the Amide III peak towards shorter wave-numbers, the most significant changes occurring in the region 1170-1000 cm^{-1} and attributed to changes in

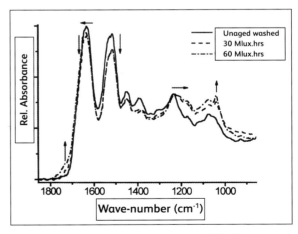

FIGURE A.6

ATR/FTIR spectra of an unaged undyed wool sample together with light aged undyed samples showing changes in the Amide I, II and III peaks and the evolution of cysteic acid at 1040cm^{-1}. (© Birbeck College)

hydrogen-bonding occurring as the keratin proteins denatured.

The chemistry of wool is dominated by the sulfur atoms of disulfide bonds between the residues of the cystine amino acid. The photo-degradation of wool in the MODHT studies caused the cystine residues to oxidise into cysteic acid residues (C-SO$_3$-) [see Fig. A.6], resulting in cystine S-monoxide and cystine S-dioxide oxidation products, as well as S-sulfonate (Bunte's salt) [see Fig. A.5].

References

1. Kellner, R., Mermet, J.-M., Otto, M. and H. M. Widmer (eds) (1998): *Infrared and Raman Spectroscopy in Analytical Chemistry* (Wiley-VCH Verlag GmbH: Weinheim), pp. 542-65.
2. Rouessac, F and A. Rouessac (2000): *Chemical Analysis, Modern Instrumentation Methods and Techniques* (John Wiley & Sons Ltd: London), pp. 161-87.
3. Woodhead, A. L., Harrigan, F. J., and J. S. Church (2005), in *The Internet Journal of Vibrational Spectroscopy* [http://www.ijvs.com/volume1/edition3/section2.html].
4. Kan C. W., Chan, K. and Y. C. W. Marcus (2003), in *AUTEX Research Journal*, vol. 3, pp. 194-205.
5. Carr, C. M. and D. M. Lewis (1993): 'An FTIR spectroscopic study of the photodegradation and thermal degradation of wool', in *Journal of Society of Dyers and Colourists*, vol. 109, pp. 21-24.

Surface Analysis

Scanning Electron Microscopy (SEM) and Energy Dispersive X-ray Microanalysis (EDX)

Electron microscopy allows high magnification imaging with excellent depth of focus of the surface topography and morphology of a sample.[1] Scanning Electron Microscopy (SEM) images are formed by scanning an electron beam across a surface and collecting electron signals from the interaction between beam and surface, for example from secondary electrons, backscattered primary electrons, Auger electrons, X-rays and light photons. Unscattered and elastically/inelastically scattered electrons pass through the sample. Some electrons are absorbed into the sample where they generate a current. This tends to happen with non-conducting samples so they are typically gold- or carbon-coated to dissipate the generated heat and charge. Magnification is achieved through the ratio of the raster scanned area on the specimen to the area on the display screen [see Figure A.7].

Each type of electronic emission brings advantages and disadvantages to the image. Secondary electrons are emitted from a small region near the sample's surface close to the primary electron beam. Their images are high resolution but low contrast compared to backscattered electron images because emissions are fewer and lower energy. Backscattered electrons are emitted from a wider and deeper region, but offer the advantage of chemical information. The number of backscattered electrons depends on the atomic number of the backscattering atoms in the region analysed: the higher the atomic number, the higher the number of backscattered electrons, resulting in a brighter image. Therefore backscattered electron images offer not only topographical

FIGURE A.7

Scanning Electron Microscopy (SEM) image of a historical metal thread. (© University of Manchester)

114

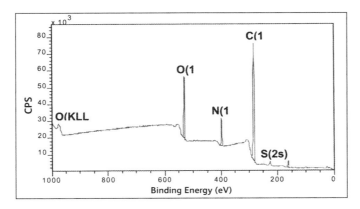

FIGURE A.8

In the XPS spectrum of unaged wool used for the MODHT studies, the main peaks are due to oxygen, nitrogen, carbon and sulphur. (© University of Manchester)

information but also chemical information through atomic number contrast.

X-rays are produced when secondary electrons are emitted from one of the orbital shells of an atom. For the atom to return to its stabilised state, an electron from a higher energy orbit fills the resulting gap. During that transition, an X-ray photon with characteristic energy and wavelength is emitted. Energy Dispersive X-ray microanalysis (EDX) allows the characteristic energy to be measured to give information about the chemical elements present on the sample surface. EDX enables compositional analysis of all elements from boron to uranium to a spatial resolution of approximately one micron.[1] The majority of X-rays are emitted from a relatively wide area, so the spatial resolution of X-ray microanalysis is relatively poor compared to even secondary electron images.

The influence of the MODHT dyeing procedures and accelerated ageing on the yarns was investigated by SEM imaging of wool and silk surfaces and cross-sections after fracture. Metal threads were also examined by SEM for manufacturing methods and corrosion morphology. EDX analysis was performed on both sides of the metal thread filaments to analyse the alloy composition and corrosion compounds. The imaging was done with a Hitachi SEM S-3000 N system equipped with a scintillator-photomultiplier type Everhart-Thornley secondary electron detector, a retractable four quadrant solid

state backscattered electron detector and a liquid nitrogen cooled EDAX Sapphire Si (Li) NL2 detector. Detector identification, sample name, working distance, accelerating voltage and the appropriate scale bar were recorded on each SEM micrograph. EDX spectra were obtained at 15 mm working distance, large aperture and at varying spot sizes and accelerating voltages (7-30 keV).

X-ray Photoelectron Spectroscopy (XPS)

XPS is a powerful, sensitive analysis technique for probing the outer surface of materials (approximately 2 nm to 10 nm depth) and providing quantitative information about atomic composition and chemical state.[2-4] The technique works by using X-ray photons to eject photoelectrons from atoms and measuring the photoelectron energies which can be specific to elements and their chemical state. The resulting spectrum for most elements is a unique set of peaks that enable their identification. The main peaks expected from XP spectra of both wool and silk correspond to oxygen O(1s) 531eV, nitrogen N(1s) 400eV, carbon C(1s) 289-285eV, and sulphur S(2p) 168-164eV [see Figure A.8].

Information about the chemical state of an element can be gained from shifts in the spectral peak positions, because an increased positive atomic charge increases the binding energy of its electrons. To correct for peak shifts caused by electrical charging of the

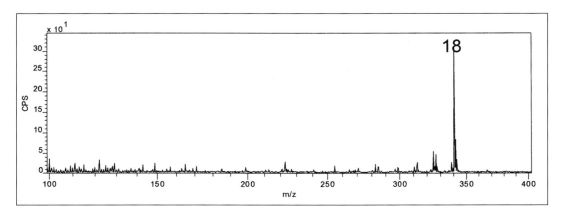

FIGURE A.9

Typical SIMS spectrum showing lipids (18 methyl eicosanoic acid, 18MEA) on an undyed, unaged wool from MODHT. (© University of Manchester)

sample during analysis, all the peaks are referenced to the C(1s) peak which, under neutral conditions, occurs at a binding energy of 285 eV.

XPS was used in MODHT to study surface chemical changes caused by accelerated and natural ageing to model and historical wool and silk fibres. Initially historic wool samples were analysed as received, but the spectra revealed significant amounts of carbon and silicon contamination so two non-swelling solvents – acetone and heptane – were assessed as cleaning agents. Heptane treatment reduced surface contamination the most (observed as a decrease in carbon and silicon signals and a signal increase for oxygen, nitrogen and sulphur), so each sample was extracted in clean glass vials at room temperature under constant agitation for 40 minutes, exchanging the heptane four times.

A Kratos Axis Ultra X-ray photoelectron spectrometer was used in the MODHT study. Wide scans of 900-0 or 600-0 eV binding energy were taken of each sample using the Al Kα mono-chromator X-ray source and resolution pass energy 160 eV. The analysed area was approximately 300 x 800 μm on all samples (lens mode hybrid and slot aperture). Other instrumental settings were 10

mA current, 15 kV anode HT, 0.4 eV step, 600-1000 ms dwell time and 1-2 sweeps per sample. High resolution survey scans of the C(1s), O(1s), N(1s), S(2p) and Al(2p) peaks were obtained using resolution pass energy 20 eV, 0.1 eV step and all other settings as above. Due to the insulating nature of wool and silk fibres, the charge neutraliser was on during all sample analyses.

Two or three different areas were analysed on each sample and the data processed using Casa XPS 2.2.67 software. Quantification was carried out using Scofield sensitivity factors and transmission functions. A linear background was used for all peaks, and if curve fitting was performed with more than one component, the full width half maximum values were constrained to differ by no more than 0.5.

Secondary Ion Mass Spectrometry (ToF-SIMS)

Secondary Ion Mass Spectrometry (SIMS) is another highly sensitive surface technique for identifying all elements and isotopes, from hydrogen to uranium, and characterising the chemical and elemental composition of a sample surface.[5-7]

In SIMS analysis, the sample surface (normally a solid) is bombarded with energetic primary particles, usually ions but electrons, neutrons or photons are also possible. Bombardment causes the emission (sputtering) of secondary particles as single atoms or molecules and molecular fragments. If the primary ion beam is repeatedly scanned across an area the surface will erode over time as the solid lattice structure is disrupted and secondary ions are ejected off the surface layers. Changes of elemental composition with depth can thus be monitored and represented as depth profile graphs of Time versus Intensity for certain elemental or molecular isotopes. This is known as Dynamic SIMS.[5-7] When the primary ion impact rate is below the accepted threshold level of 1×10^{13} ions cm^{-2}, the technique examines a stable surface and the method is known as Static SIMS.

SIMS analysis was carried out to study the influence of dyeing procedures and accelerated and natural ageing on wool and silk, in particular lipid removal and sulphur oxidation on the wool surfaces [see Figure A.9]. Dynamic SIMS was employed for surface analysis and depth profiling of metal thread filaments for the investigation of manufacturing technique and corrosion products.

SIMS spectra of wool and silk surfaces were obtained in positive and negative ion mode in a mass range of 0 to 1000 using a PHI 7000 instrument. Analysis was performed under static conditions using a Cs^+ primary ion source, operated at 8 keV with a pulse length of 1.25 ns. A pulsed electron flood source (50-70 eV) was used for charge compensation. Typical acquisition times were 95 s. Further analyses of wool surfaces were carried out on an ION-TOF ToF-SIMS 5 instrument equipped with a bismuth primary ion source. High resolution mass spectra were collected from sample areas measuring 0.1 mm x 0.1 mm using Bi_3^+ ion bombardment.

The data was processed using Casa XPS 2.2.67 software. All spectra were calibrated from time bins to mass bins using the CH and C_2H peak positions for negative ion spectra, and CH_3 and C_2H_3 peak positions for positive ion spectra. Semi-quantification was performed by measuring relative peak areas.

Dynamic SIMS analysis was performed on a CAMECA IMS 4f Magnetic Sector SIMS instrument. The Cs^+ primary ion beam was operated at 10 keV, with a beam current of 1 nA and for depth profiles 2 nA to 15 nA. The areas analysed were approximately 200 x 200 µm. Typical acquisition times were 200 s to 400 s for spectra and 1000 s to 4000 s for depth profiles, depending on the achieved analysis depth. A reference crater was measured using a Dektak Profilometer; subsequent depth calibrations were made based on the reference crater measurement, using a sputter rate factor. The approximate subsurface analytical depth was 0.25 µm to 2 µm.

References

1. Goldstein, J. I., D. E. Newbury, P. Echlin, D. C. Joy, C. Fiori and E. Lifshin (1981): *Scanning Electron Microscopy and X-Ray Microanalysis* (Plenum Press: New York, London).
2. Briggs, D. (1998): *Surface Analysis of Polymers by XPS and Static SIMS* (University Press, Cambridge), pp 14-47.
3. Moulder, J. F., W. F. Stickle, P. E. Sobol and K. D. Bomben (1992, 1995): *Handbook of X-ray Photoelectron Spectroscopy* (Physical Electronics, Inc., Eden Prairie, Minnesota), pp. 9-33, 128.
4. Watts, F. J. (1990): *An Introduction to Surface Analysis by Electron Spectroscopy* (Oxford University Press: Royal Microscopical Society), pp. 1-23.
5. Briggs, D., A. Brown and J. C. Vickerman (1989): Handbook of Static Secondary Ion Mass Spectroscopy (John Wiley & Sons), pp. 3-15.
6. Cherepin, V. T. (1987): Secondary Ion Mass Spectroscopy of Solid Surfaces (VNU Science Press BV, Utrecht), pp. 1-92.
7. Vickerman, J. C., A. Brown and N. M. Reed (eds) (1989): *Secondary Ion Mass Spectroscopy. Principles and Applications. The International Series of Monographs on Chemistry* (Clarendon Press: Oxford), p. 22.

APPENDIX 2

Dyeing Recipes

Marei Hacke and Anita Quye

The following are the dyeing recipes for the model tapestries made for the project. Dyed fabric remaining when the project ended was divided into three and deposited with the scientists at three project partner institutions: Historic Royal Palaces, Royal Institute for Cultural Heritage (KIK) and National Museums Scotland. Sample requests for research to further historical textile preservation and investigation are welcomed.

Silk mordants

Boil mordant

438g alum dissolved in 57L boiling water. 10 hanks (1140g) added and boiled for 10 min, then removed. The liquor left to cool to ambient before re-immersing the hanks for 10 hrs.

Semelwater (for wool and silk RS1)

2kg wheat bran to 45L water and brought to the boil. The heat turned off and a further 30L of water added. The vat covered and stirred at 7 x 1 hr intervals on Day 1.

After 6 days, 40L removed for Red S1 and replaced with 40 L of hot water, then the vat stirred and left for another 24 hrs. Of this, 70L used for Red W 1.

For BS1

See dyeing recipe for **Brown Silk OGS: Oak Galls**

For YS1 and first mordant for YS3

385g alum dissolved in hot water, then added to 50L water at approximately 40°C. 9 hanks (1025g) immersed for 20 hrs, then rinsed. 3 hanks dried for YS3.

For YS2

225g alum dissolved in 30L water at approximately 40°C. 11 hanks (600g) immersed for 2 hrs.

First mordant for RS1

315g alum dissolved in hot water, then cold water added to make up to 150L. 10 hanks (1260g) immersed for 16 hrs, then rinsed. 5 hanks dried and used for RS1 and the remaining 5 as analytical controls.

Second mordant for RS1

315g alum dissolved in hot water, then made up to 85L with cold water (final temperature 35°C approximately). 5 unmordanted hanks plus 5 hanks from first brazilwood dye bath immersed for 16 hrs, then drained and wrung.

For RS2

210g alum dissolved in boiling water, then cold water added to make up to 50L (approx. temperature 50°C). 8 hanks (842g) immersed for 20 hrs, then rinsed. 2 hanks dried and the remaining 6 used for RS2.

For RS3

267g alum and 67g sodium chloride dissolved in 50L boiling water. 1kg copper turnings added and the heat turned off. 5 hanks (534g) immersed and left for 24hrs before rinsing.

118

For YW1

23g alum dissolved in 75L boiling water. 8 hanks (1.5 kg) immersed, boiled for 2hrs, then wrung out.

For YW2

15g alum dissolved in 75L boiling water. 6 hanks (1kg) immersed, boiled for 2hrs, then wrung out and left to dry.

For RW1

150g alum dissolved in 50L of semelwater. 6 hanks (1 kg) immersed, boiled for 2hrs, then drained (not wrung).

First mordant for RW2

70g oak galls added to 50L boiling water and boiled for 30 mins. 4 hanks (700g) immersed and boiled for 2 hrs, then drained but not wrung.

Second mordant for RW2

35g alum dissolved in 50L boiling water. 4 hanks from first mordanting immersed and boiled for 2hrs, then drained and wrung.

For RW3

105g alum dissolved in 35L boiling water. 4 hanks immersed and boiled for 1.5 hrs, then excess liquid squeezed out.

For RW4 and RW5

106g alum, 69g tartaric acid and 31g sodium chloride dissolved in 50L boiling water. 31g sandalwood added, then 8 hanks (1340g) immersed and boiled for 2 hrs. The heat turned off and the bath left to cool for 24 hrs. The hanks removed, but not wrung. 4 hanks used for RW4 and the remaining 4 for RW5.

For BW1 and BW2

8 hanks (1.3 kg) immersed in 50L water at 75°C then removed before adding 1.3 kg oak galls and bringing to the boil. All wet hanks re-immersed and boiled for 2 hrs, then drained, cooled down, rinsed with hot water and left to dry.

For Blank and Blank with lye

75g potassium carbonate dissolved in 75L water. 8 hanks (1.3 kg) immersed and boiled for 2 hrs before removing and drying.

For BW3

See dyeing recipe for
Brown Wool ABW: Alder Bark

For Alum

150g alum dissolved in 50L water. 4 pre-wetted hanks (670g) immersed and boiled for 1.5 hrs before wringing, rinsing and drying.

Wool mordants

Washed wool

> **Washed**
>
> Wool was washed twice in excess water at 80°C for 20 mins.

Blank dyed wool

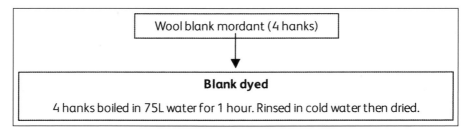

Wool blank mordant (4 hanks)

Blank dyed

4 hanks boiled in 75L water for 1 hour. Rinsed in cold water then dried.

Blank dyed wool with lye

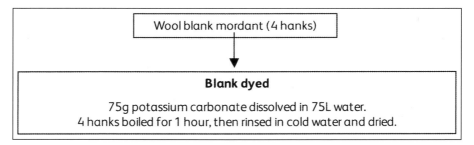

Wool blank mordant (4 hanks)

Blank dyed

75g potassium carbonate dissolved in 75L water.
4 hanks boiled for 1 hour, then rinsed in cold water and dried.

Yellow silk YS1: weld

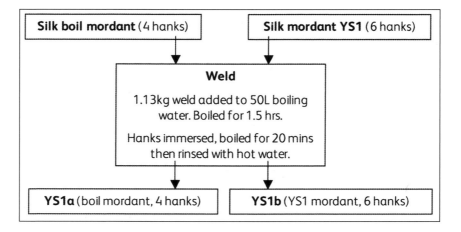

Silk boil mordant (4 hanks)   Silk mordant YS1 (6 hanks)

Weld

1.13kg weld added to 50L boiling water. Boiled for 1.5 hrs.

Hanks immersed, boiled for 20 mins then rinsed with hot water.

YS1a (boil mordant, 4 hanks)   **YS1b** (YS1 mordant, 6 hanks)

Yellow silk YS2: young fustic

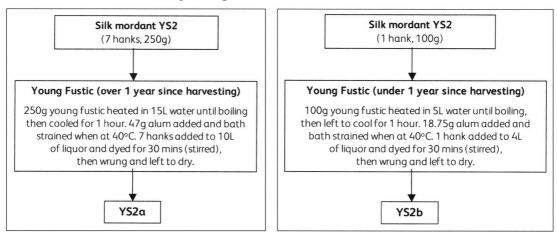

Silk mordant YS2
(7 hanks, 250g)

↓

Young Fustic (over 1 year since harvesting)

250g young fustic heated in 15L water until boiling then cooled for 1 hour. 47g alum added and bath strained when at 40°C. 7 hanks added to 10L of liquor and dyed for 30 mins (stirred), then wrung and left to dry.

↓

YS2a

Silk mordant YS2
(1 hank, 100g)

↓

Young Fustic (under 1 year since harvesting)

100g young fustic heated in 5L water until boiling, then left to cool for 1 hour. 18.75g alum added and bath strained when at 40°C. 1 hank added to 4L of liquor and dyed for 30 mins (stirred), then wrung and left to dry.

↓

YS2b

Yellow silk YS3: dyer's greenweed (see page 122)

Green silk GS2: woad and weld

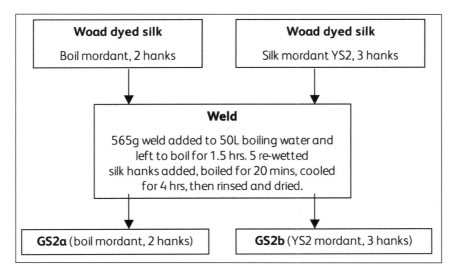

Woad dyed silk

Boil mordant, 2 hanks

Woad dyed silk

Silk mordant YS2, 3 hanks

↓ ↓

Weld

565g weld added to 50L boiling water and left to boil for 1.5 hrs. 5 re-wetted silk hanks added, boiled for 20 mins, cooled for 4 hrs, then rinsed and dried.

↓ ↓

GS2a (boil mordant, 2 hanks)   **GS2b** (YS2 mordant, 3 hanks)

Yellow silk YS3: dyer's greenweed

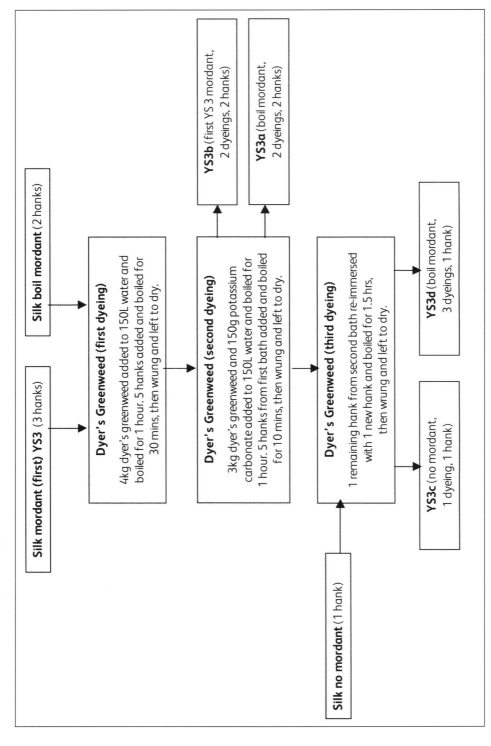

Silk boil mordant (2 hanks)

Silk mordant (first) YS3 (3 hanks)

Dyer's Greenweed (first dyeing)

4kg dyer's greenweed added to 150L water and boiled for 1 hour. 5 hanks added and boiled for 30 mins, then wrung and left to dry.

Dyer's Greenweed (second dyeing)

3kg dyer's greenweed and 150g potassium carbonate added to 150L water and boiled for 1 hour. 5 hanks from first bath added and boiled for 10 mins, then wrung and left to dry.

Dyer's Greenweed (third dyeing)

1 remaining hank from second bath re-immersed with 1 new hank and boiled for 1.5 hrs, then wrung and left to dry.

YS3b (first YS 3 mordant, 2 dyeings, 2 hanks)

YS3a (boil mordant, 2 dyeings, 2 hanks)

YS3d (boil mordant, 3 dyeings, 1 hank)

YS3c (no mordant, 1 dyeing, 1 hank)

Silk no mordant (1 hank)

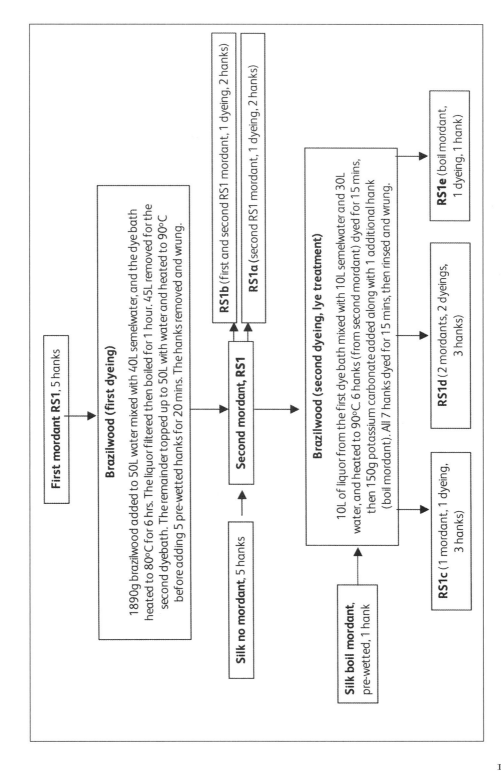

Red silk RS1: brazilwood

First mordant RS1, 5 hanks

Brazilwood (first dyeing)

1890g brazilwood added to 50L water mixed with 40L semelwater, and the dye bath heated to 80°C for 6 hrs. The liquor filtered then boiled for 1 hour. 45L removed for the second dyebath. The remainder topped up to 50L with water and heated to 90°C before adding 5 pre-wetted hanks for 20 mins. The hanks removed and wrung.

Second mordant, RS1

Silk no mordant, 5 hanks

RS1b (first and second RS1 mordant, 1 dyeing, 2 hanks)

RS1a (second RS1 mordant, 1 dyeing, 2 hanks)

Brazilwood (second dyeing, lye treatment)

10L of liquor from the first dye bath mixed with 10L semelwater and 30L water, and heated to 90°C. 6 hanks (from second mordant) dyed for 15 mins, then 150g potassium carbonate added along with 1 additional hank (boil mordant). All 7 hanks dyed for 15 mins, then rinsed and wrung.

Silk boil mordant, pre-wetted, 1 hank

RS1c (1 mordant, 1 dyeing, 3 hanks)

RS1d (2 mordants, 2 dyeings, 3 hanks)

RS1e (boil mordant, 1 dyeing, 1 hank)

Red silk RS2: madder

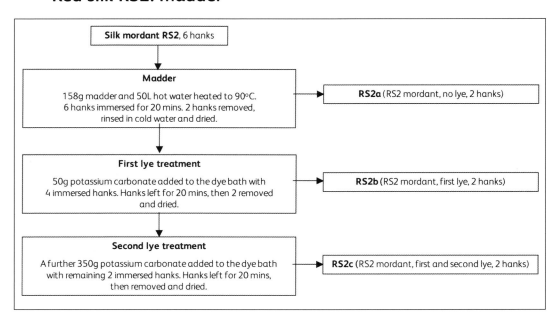

Silk mordant RS2, 6 hanks

Madder

158g madder and 50L hot water heated to 90°C.
6 hanks immersed for 20 mins. 2 hanks removed,
rinsed in cold water and dried.

RS2a (RS2 mordant, no lye, 2 hanks)

First lye treatment

50g potassium carbonate added to the dye bath with
4 immersed hanks. Hanks left for 20 mins, then 2 removed
and dried.

RS2b (RS2 mordant, first lye, 2 hanks)

Second lye treatment

A further 350g potassium carbonate added to the dye bath
with remaining 2 immersed hanks. Hanks left for 20 mins,
then removed and dried.

RS2c (RS2 mordant, first and second lye, 2 hanks)

Red silk RS3: cochineal

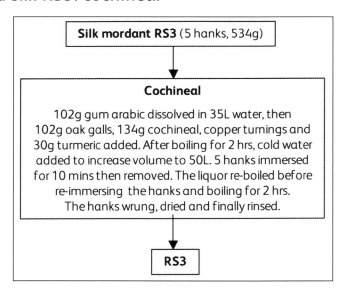

Silk mordant RS3 (5 hanks, 534g)

Cochineal

102g gum arabic dissolved in 35L water, then
102g oak galls, 134g cochineal, copper turnings and
30g turmeric added. After boiling for 2 hrs, cold water
added to increase volume to 50L. 5 hanks immersed
for 10 mins then removed. The liquor re-boiled before
re-immersing the hanks and boiling for 2 hrs.
The hanks wrung, dried and finally rinsed.

RS3

BS1 mordant and brown silk OGS: oak galls

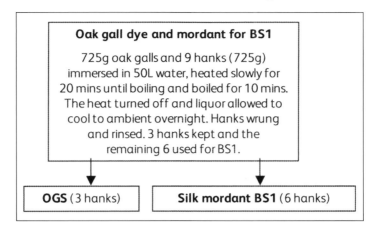

Oak gall dye and mordant for BS1

725g oak galls and 9 hanks (725g) immersed in 50L water, heated slowly for 20 mins until boiling and boiled for 10 mins. The heat turned off and liquor allowed to cool to ambient overnight. Hanks wrung and rinsed. 3 hanks kept and the remaining 6 used for BS1.

OGS (3 hanks)   **Silk mordant BS1** (6 hanks)

Black silk BS1: iron sulfate

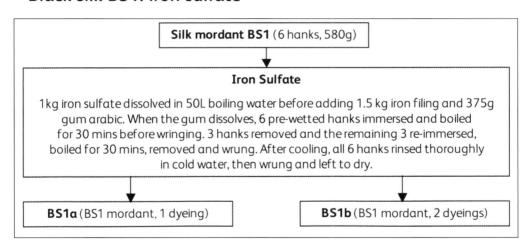

Silk mordant BS1 (6 hanks, 580g)

Iron Sulfate

1kg iron sulfate dissolved in 50L boiling water before adding 1.5 kg iron filing and 375g gum arabic. When the gum dissolves, 6 pre-wetted hanks immersed and boiled for 30 mins before wringing. 3 hanks removed and the remaining 3 re-immersed, boiled for 30 mins, removed and wrung. After cooling, all 6 hanks rinsed thoroughly in cold water, then wrung and left to dry.

BS1a (BS1 mordant, 1 dyeing)   **BS1b** (BS1 mordant, 2 dyeings)

Blue silk and wool: woad

| Silk, degummed (5 hanks) | Wool, scoured (3 hanks) | Silk, YS1a (boil mordant, 2 hanks) | Silk, YS1a (boil mordant, 2 hanks) | Silk, YS1b (weld dye, alum mordant, 3 hanks) | Wool YW1 (weld dye, alum mordant, 3 hanks) |

| Wool, alum mordant (3 hanks) | Silk, alum mordant (3 hanks) | Silk, boil mordant (2 hanks) |

Woad

2 kg (total) couched woad in a 30L water. Vat created by reduction with bacterial action at 45 to 50°C. Wood ash and lime were used to maintain pH 8.2–8.5.

Blue yarns

Green yarns (see GW2 individual recipes)

Yellow wool YW1: weld

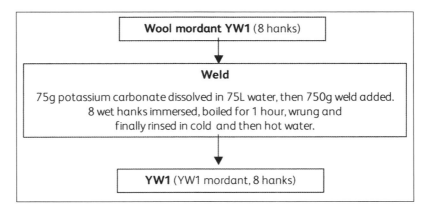

Wool mordant YW1 (8 hanks)

Weld

75g potassium carbonate dissolved in 75L water, then 750g weld added. 8 wet hanks immersed, boiled for 1 hour, wrung and finally rinsed in cold and then hot water.

YW1 (YW1 mordant, 8 hanks)

Yellow wool YW2: dyer's greenweed

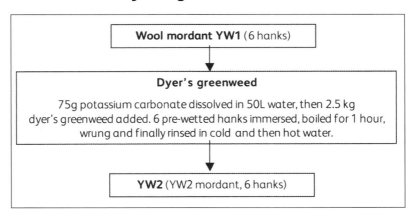

Wool mordant YW1 (6 hanks)

Dyer's greenweed

75g potassium carbonate dissolved in 50L water, then 2.5 kg dyer's greenweed added. 6 pre-wetted hanks immersed, boiled for 1 hour, wrung and finally rinsed in cold and then hot water.

YW2 (YW2 mordant, 6 hanks)

Red wool RW1: madder

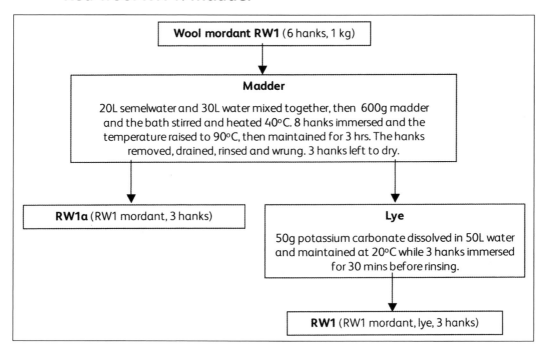

Wool mordant RW1 (6 hanks, 1 kg)

Madder

20L semelwater and 30L water mixed together, then 600g madder and the bath stirred and heated 40°C. 8 hanks immersed and the temperature raised to 90°C, then maintained for 3 hrs. The hanks removed, drained, rinsed and wrung. 3 hanks left to dry.

RW1a (RW1 mordant, 3 hanks)

Lye

50g potassium carbonate dissolved in 50L water and maintained at 20°C while 3 hanks immersed for 30 mins before rinsing.

RW1 (RW1 mordant, lye, 3 hanks)

Red wool RW2: madder and oak galls

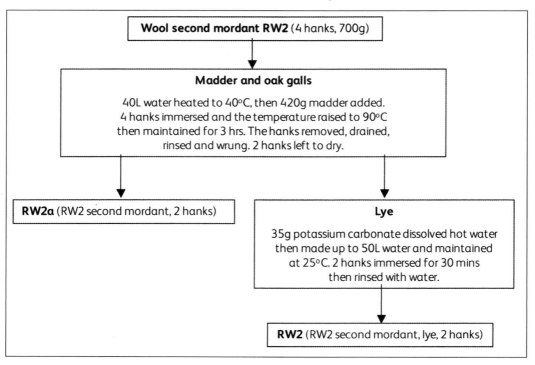

Wool second mordant RW2 (4 hanks, 700g)

Madder and oak galls

40L water heated to 40°C, then 420g madder added. 4 hanks immersed and the temperature raised to 90°C then maintained for 3 hrs. The hanks removed, drained, rinsed and wrung. 2 hanks left to dry.

RW2a (RW2 second mordant, 2 hanks)

Lye

35g potassium carbonate dissolved hot water then made up to 50L water and maintained at 25°C. 2 hanks immersed for 30 mins then rinsed with water.

RW2 (RW2 second mordant, lye, 2 hanks)

Red wool RW3: brazilwood

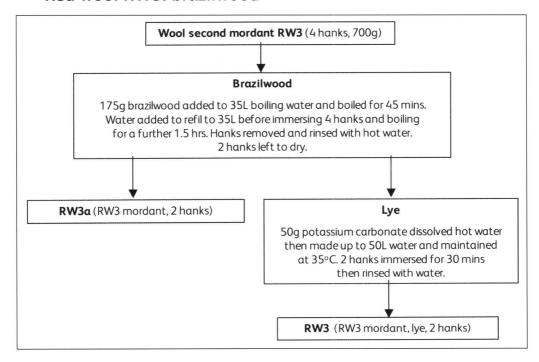

Wool second mordant RW3 (4 hanks, 700g)

Brazilwood

175g brazilwood added to 35L boiling water and boiled for 45 mins. Water added to refil to 35L before immersing 4 hanks and boiling for a further 1.5 hrs. Hanks removed and rinsed with hot water. 2 hanks left to dry.

RW3a (RW3 mordant, 2 hanks)

Lye

50g potassium carbonate dissolved hot water then made up to 50L water and maintained at 35°C. 2 hanks immersed for 30 mins then rinsed with water.

RW3 (RW3 mordant, lye, 2 hanks)

Red wool RW4: cochineal

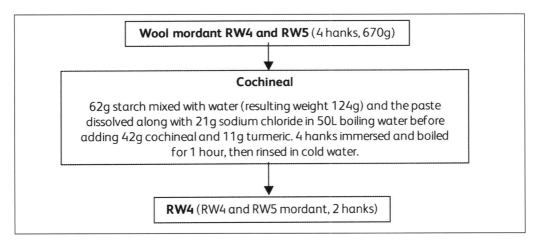

Wool mordant RW4 and RW5 (4 hanks, 670g)

Cochineal

62g starch mixed with water (resulting weight 124g) and the paste dissolved along with 21g sodium chloride in 50L boiling water before adding 42g cochineal and 11g turmeric. 4 hanks immersed and boiled for 1 hour, then rinsed in cold water.

RW4 (RW4 and RW5 mordant, 2 hanks)

Red wool RW5: cochineal and alum

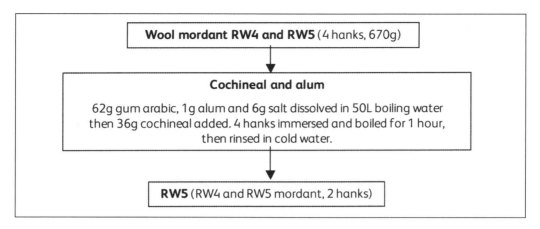

Wool mordant RW4 and RW5 (4 hanks, 670g)

Cochineal and alum

62g gum arabic, 1g alum and 6g salt dissolved in 50L boiling water then 36g cochineal added. 4 hanks immersed and boiled for 1 hour, then rinsed in cold water.

RW5 (RW4 and RW5 mordant, 2 hanks)

Black wool BW1: iron sulfate

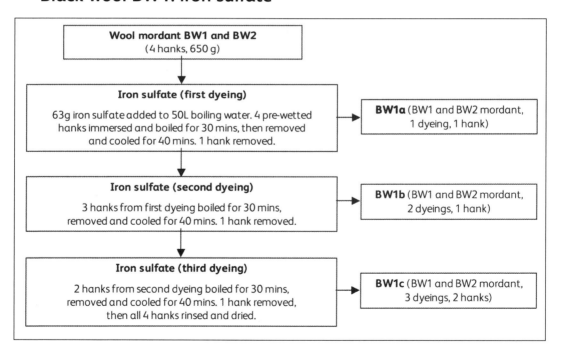

Wool mordant BW1 and BW2
(4 hanks, 650 g)

Iron sulfate (first dyeing)

63g iron sulfate added to 50L boiling water. 4 pre-wetted hanks immersed and boiled for 30 mins, then removed and cooled for 40 mins. 1 hank removed.

BW1a (BW1 and BW2 mordant, 1 dyeing, 1 hank)

Iron sulfate (second dyeing)

3 hanks from first dyeing boiled for 30 mins, removed and cooled for 40 mins. 1 hank removed.

BW1b (BW1 and BW2 mordant, 2 dyeings, 1 hank)

Iron sulfate (third dyeing)

2 hanks from second dyeing boiled for 30 mins, removed and cooled for 40 mins. 1 hank removed, then all 4 hanks rinsed and dried.

BW1c (BW1 and BW2 mordant, 3 dyeings, 2 hanks)

Black wool BW2: iron sulfate (increased amount)

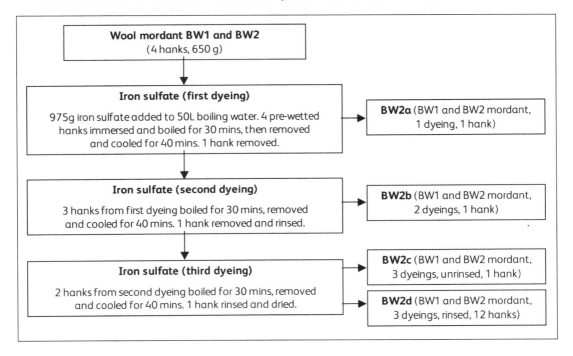

Wool mordant BW1 and BW2
(4 hanks, 650 g)

Iron sulfate (first dyeing)

975g iron sulfate added to 50L boiling water. 4 pre-wetted hanks immersed and boiled for 30 mins, then removed and cooled for 40 mins. 1 hank removed.

BW2a (BW1 and BW2 mordant, 1 dyeing, 1 hank)

Iron sulfate (second dyeing)

3 hanks from first dyeing boiled for 30 mins, removed and cooled for 40 mins. 1 hank removed and rinsed.

BW2b (BW1 and BW2 mordant, 2 dyeings, 1 hank)

Iron sulfate (third dyeing)

2 hanks from second dyeing boiled for 30 mins, removed and cooled for 40 mins. 1 hank rinsed and dried.

BW2c (BW1 and BW2 mordant, 3 dyeings, unrinsed, 1 hank)

BW2d (BW1 and BW2 mordant, 3 dyeings, rinsed, 12 hanks)

Green wool GW2: woad and weld

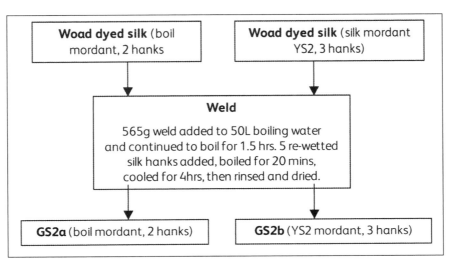

Woad dyed silk (boil mordant, 2 hanks

Woad dyed silk (silk mordant YS2, 3 hanks)

Weld

565g weld added to 50L boiling water and continued to boil for 1.5 hrs. 5 re-wetted silk hanks added, boiled for 20 mins, cooled for 4hrs, then rinsed and dried.

GS2a (boil mordant, 2 hanks)

GS2b (YS2 mordant, 3 hanks)

BW3 mordant and brown wool ABW: alder bark

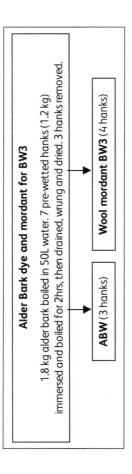

Alder Bark dye and mordant for BW3

1.8 kg alder bark boiled in 50L water. 7 pre-wetted hanks (1.2 kg) immersed and boiled for 2hrs, then drained, wrung and dried. 3 hanks removed.

ABW (3 hanks)

Wool mordant BW3 (4 hanks)

Black wool BW3: iron sulfate and alder bark

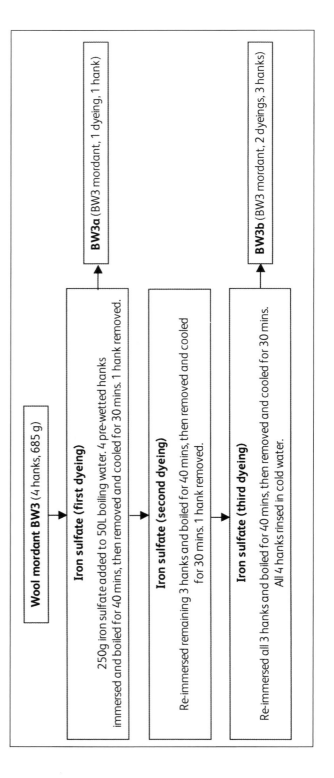

Wool mordant BW3 (4 hanks, 685 g)

Iron sulfate (first dyeing)

250g iron sulfate added to 50L boiling water. 4 pre-wetted hanks immersed and boiled for 40 mins, then removed and cooled for 30 mins. 1 hank removed.

Iron sulfate (second dyeing)

Re-immersed remaining 3 hanks and boiled for 40 mins, then removed and cooled for 30 mins. 1 hank removed.

Iron sulfate (third dyeing)

Re-immersed all 3 hanks and boiled for 40 mins, then removed and cooled for 30 mins. All 4 hanks rinsed in cold water.

BW3a (BW3 mordant, 1 dyeing, 1 hank)

BW3b (BW3 mordant, 2 dyeings, 3 hanks)

BW4 mordant and brown wool OGW: oak gall

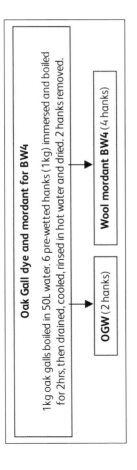

Oak Gall dye and mordant for BW4

1kg oak galls boiled in 50L water. 6 pre-wetted hanks (1kg) immersed and boiled for 2hrs, then drained, cooled, rinsed in hot water and dried. 2 hanks removed.

OGW (2 hanks)

Wool mordant BW4 (4 hanks)

Black wool BW4: iron sulfate and copper sulfate

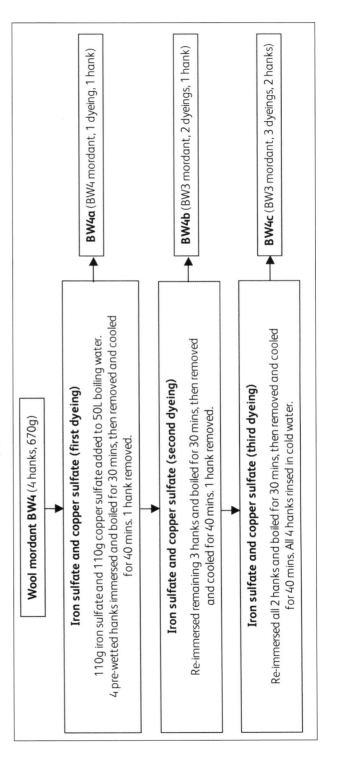

Wool mordant BW4 (4 hanks, 670g)

Iron sulfate and copper sulfate (first dyeing)

110g iron sulfate and 110g copper sulfate added to 50L boiling water. 4 pre-wetted hanks immersed and boiled for 30 mins, then removed and cooled for 40 mins. 1 hank removed.

Iron sulfate and copper sulfate (second dyeing)

Re-immersed remaining 3 hanks and boiled for 30 mins, then removed and cooled for 40 mins. 1 hank removed.

Iron sulfate and copper sulfate (third dyeing)

Re-immersed all 2 hanks and boiled for 30 mins, then removed and cooled for 40 mins. All 4 hanks rinsed in cold water.

BW4a (BW4 mordant, 1 dyeing, 1 hank)

BW4b (BW3 mordant, 2 dyeings, 1 hank)

BW4c (BW3 mordant, 3 dyeings, 2 hanks)

Bibliography

Basic bibliography on the collections studied during the MODHT project:

ARMINJON, C. (2004): 'Les saints de choeur. Tentures médiévales et Renaissance', in *L'Estampille-l'Objet d'Art*, no. 392, Juin, pp. 60-69.

BUCHANAN, I. (1999): 'The tapestries acquired by King Philip II in the Netherlands in 1549-50 and 1555-59: new documentation', in *Gazette des Beaux-Arts*, vol. 134, Octobre, pp. 131-52.

CALBERT, F. A. (1921): *The Spanish royal tapestries* (London/New York).

CAMPBELL, T. P. (1994): 'William III and "The Triumph of Lust": the tapestries hung in the King's State Apartments in 1699', in *Apollo*, no. 390, pp. 22-31.

CAMPBELL, T. P. (2002): *Tapestry in the Renaissance. Art and Magnificence* (New York: The Metropolitan Museum of Art).

CAMPBELL, T. P. (2007): *Henry VIII and the Art of Majesty. Tapestries at the Tudor Court* (New Haven and London: The Paul Mellan Centre for Studies in British Art by Yale University Press).

CRICK-KUNTZIGER, M. (1956): *Catalogue des Tapisseries (XIVe au XVIIIe siècle)* (Bruxelles: Musées Royaux d'Art et d'Histoire).

CROOK Y NAVARROT, J. (1903): 'Conde de Valencia de Don Juan', *Tapices de la Corona de España* (Madrid: Hauser y Menet), vol. 2.

DELMARCEL, G. (1977-79): *Tapisseries, 1. Moyen Age et première Renaissance. 2. Renaissance et Maniérisme. 3. Baroque et XVIIIe siècle. Guide du visiteur* (Bruxelles: Musées Royaux d'Art et d'Historie).

DELMARCEL, G. (1999): *Flemish Tapestry from the 15th to the 18th Century* (Tielt: Lanoo).

DELMARCEL, G. and DUVERGER, E. (1987): *Bruges et la tapisserie* (Mouscron-Bruges).

DIGBY, G. W. (1980): *The Tapestry Collection. Medieval and Renaissance* (London: Her Majesty's Stationery Office).

GÖBEL, H. (1923): *Wandteppiche I. Theil. Die Niederlande* (Leipzig: Verlag von Klinkhardt & Biermann), vol. 2.

HERRERO, C. (1994): 'Las tapicerías ricas del Alcázar de Madrid', *El Real Alcázar de Madrid. Dos siglos de arquitectura y coleccionismo en la Corte de los Reyes de España* (Madrid: Nerea).

HERRERO, C. (2000): *Catálogo de Tapices del Patrimonio Nacional. III. Siglo XVIII. Reinado de Felipe V* (Madrid: Patrimonio Nacional).

HERRERO, C. (2004): *Tapices de Isabel la Católica. Origen de la colección real española. Tapestries of Isabella the Catholic. Origin of the Spanish royal collection* (Madrid: Patrimonio Nacional).

JUNQUERA DE VEGA, P., HERRERO CARRETERO, C. and DÍAZ GALLEGOS, C. (1986): *Catálogo de Tapices del Patrimonio Nacional. Siglos XVI y XVII.* (Madrid), vols I and II.

JOUBERT, F., LEFEBURE, A. and BERTRAND, P. F. (1995): *Histoire de la Tapisserie. En Europe, du Moyen Âge à nos jours.* (Paris: Flammarion).

MARILLIER, H. C. (1951): *The tapestries at Hampton Court Palace* (London).

SWAIN, M. (1988): *Tapestries and textiles at the Palace of Holyroodhouse in the Royal Collection* (Edinburgh, London).

[TAPISSERIES] (1976): *Tapisseries bruxelloises de la pré-Renaissance*, DELMARCEL, G. (ed.) (Bruxelles: Musées Royaux d'Art et d'Histoire).

THOMSON, W. G. (1906): *A History of Tapestry from the Earliest Times until the Present Day* (London: Hodder & Stoughton).

TORMO, E. and SÁNCHEZ CANTÓN, F. J. (1919): *Los tapices de la Casa del Rey Nuestro Señor* (Madrid: Gráficas Mateu).

WAUTERS, A. (1878): *Les tapisseries bruxelloises. Essai historique sur les Tapisseries et tapissiers de haute et basse-lice de Bruxelles* (Bruxelles: Imp. de Ve. Julien Baertsoen).

WEIGERT, L. (2004): *Weaving Sacred Stories. French Choir Tapestries and the Performance of Clerical Identity* (Ithaca: Cornell University Press).